Ultimate Garages

Phil Berg

MOTORBOOKS
INTERNATIONAL

Dedication

To Joanie, who enthusiastically became a single parent to Elizabeth and Erik while papa hunted garages.

This edition first published in 2003 by Motorbooks International, an imprint of MBI Publishing Company, Galtier Plaza, Suite 200, 380 Jackson Street, St. Paul, MN 55101-3885 USA

Motorbooks International titles are also available at discounts in bulk quantity for industrial or sales-promotional use. For details write to Special Sales Manager at Motorbooks International Wholesalers & Distributors, Galtier Plaza, Suite 200, 380 Jackson Street, St. Paul, MN 55101-3885 USA.

ISBN 0-7603-1471-3

On the front cover: Ken Gross stores almost 100 intake manifolds for Ford V-8 engines and a collection of classic cars in his spacious three-car garage. *Michael Stewart*

On the frontispiece: Architect Dan Scully considers his garage, designed to look like an engine block, a shrine dedicated to the gods of fuel, speed, and racers. *Jeff Hackett*

On the title page: After the sun sets on Stanley Gold's garage, all his special Porsches, including a rare Porsche farm tractor, reflect in the backyard pool. *Phil Berg*

On the back cover: Dean Stanley designed his small, idyllic garage using Japanese-inspired space-saving techniques. *Phil Berg*

Endpapers: Tom Sparks' garage is filled with one-of-a-kind cars, including several that have been featured in movies. *Phil Berg*

Acquisitions Editor: Lee Klancher
Project Editor: Leah Cochenet Noel
Designed by Tom Heffron

Printed in China

Contents

Preface 6

Part 1 **The Garage as a Palace**

Candy Store
A Clubhouse for Cars 13

Stanley Gold
Pride of Porsches 21

Walter Hill
It Started with One Car 31

Jay Leno
Projects Expand to Fit the Space 41

Bruce Massman
A Home for the Antiques 53

Bruce Meyer
Meet Mister Garage 63

Peter Mullin
Blending Art and Cars 71

David Sydorick
A Place for Centerpiece Cars 79

Al Wiseman
Classic Car Castle 89

Part 2 **Real-World Garages**

Ken Gross
A New Start 99

Bill Hammerstein
The Fun Run Place 105

Chuck Higgins
A Workaholic's Vision 113

Peter McCoy
A Classy Workshop 121

Lynn Park
A Place for a Fanatic 129

Buddy Pepp
Portrait of a Car Family 139

Don Sherman
Hobby Meets Business 149

Tom Sparks
Studio Collection 157

Dean Stanley
Cozy Quarters for Cars 167

Part 3 **Nontraditional Garages**

Curt Catallo
A Magic Vision for Car Space 177

Horsepower TV
Locked Inside for a Week 185

Mark Lambert
The Preservationist 193

Dan Scully
A Shrine to the Gods of Fuel 201

Guy Webster
Brand New Old Barn 209

Brock Yates
Parking in History's Shadow 217

Index 224

Preface

Because it is impractical to drive forever, we car people have to park somewhere. This is where.

It is a universal law that the wife must decorate the house and the husband is allowed the basement and the garage. It may be an unwritten law, perhaps only enforced in the various Midwestern states where I've lived, but it's as solid a piece of human legislature as has ever been devised.

Aside from the chauvinism, this is a good law, at least to car and motorcycle nuts. We enthusiasts tend to live in garages, because, well, that's where our vehicles are. The places in this book are where we wish to spend our time—focused on the functional art inside and pondering the artifacts of extraordinary designers, talented craftsmen, and creative engineers. We can't get enough, so it's probably a good thing that local building codes usually prohibit sleeping in garages.

The idea for this book has been inside the heads of several real car nuts for years. Veteran auto magazine art director Larry Crane has been to a number of the garages you will see here, and he gave me enough juicy details about what was inside them that I couldn't wait to visit.

Ken Gross opened the doors to let me inside the most serious collectors' garages, and Bill Hammerstein, in the spirit of true Midwestern values, vouched for me to collectors, who with nothing more than "Hammer's" word, allowed me to stumble around alone with their irreplaceable possessions. Expert classic car photographer Dennis Adler in fact began shooting some of these garages before this book was in the making. Irrepressibly car crazy Bill Warner led me to several wonderful places, too. These guys all speak garage fluently.

I started paying attention to ultimate garages after developing a January 1998 article as a senior editor for *Car and Driver* magazine. The article, titled "Garagemahals," reflected a solicitation from the magazine requesting snapshots of readers' garages. While the results were interesting—someone had turned part of his garage into a 1950s sock hop style–diner, the serious car people weren't included. So I started asking people I knew about their favorite garages. Within weeks I had a list of more than 50 places.

The Corvette and the Buick Skymaster are the cars that Sparks likes to use most. Phil Berg

As I visited these places, I quickly got the sense none of these car and motorcycle collectors think of themselves as having possessions. They consider themselves as foster parents, entrusted with the care of the special vehicles in their garages. Yet these enthusiasts don't lock the vehicles up in the padded cells of a museum or gallery. Instead, they drive them on the road at speed. They get their hands dirty keeping them fit.

They've built these impressive structures to allow their car hospitality to manifest.

Little details caught my eyes: Dean Stanley's compact garage has more than 80 electrical outlets, and each plywood-covered wall panel is caulked and each door weather-stripped, sealing the cars inside. Hospital operating rooms let in more germs. Chuck Higgins' four-car garage needed 30,000 nails to construct, and he shot

Mark Lambert's garage, an old a fire station, was built from stone and masonry. The original wooden firehouse burned down while the fire crew was on a run. Phil Berg

each nail himself, tossing the empty nail cartons into a pile that stayed where it was until the garage was finished. While Al Wiseman may have up to 125 cars in his personal garage, he also has collected 150 antique tire pressure gauges, one at a time. Jay Leno built a second building next to his airplane hangar to store his Duesenberg collection because he couldn't wait for his neighbor to sell him a second hangar. When the day eventually came that his neighbor offered to sell him the building, he jumped on the deal and ended up with a total of three buildings, which bulge at the seams to hold his 80-car collection—all ready to drive at a moment's notice.

Until he got married, Mark Lambert spent six years living in his garage—an unrestored 1930 firehouse. Lynn Park found a truckload of antique Colorado barn wood and stored it until he built his 12-car California garage, where he used the wood for the inside walls. He also learned how to find a good mounted buffalo head, which hangs in his garage above his Cobras. He didn't mount the head because he yearns for the Ponderosa, but because he says buffalo are so American, like his cars. Some of the special Jaguars Walter Hill owns are not legal to drive on the street, so he built his own driving course on the airfield adjacent to his garage.

For every garage you see here, there are hundreds more that fill the role of ultimate refuge for our fellow car nuts. The collection of buildings in this book is intended to give a broad look at a range of places car people go when they're not driving. It only scratches the surface, however. Many garages I visited are not in this book, the owners being understandably not convinced that they should give up their privacy. The folks at the Candy Store made me swear on a stack of Chilton manuals never to reveal their location. The folks who did invite me into their garages to share some time with them, their vehicles, and offer their thoughts about their car passions were as fascinating as their car havens. The garages, all of which I found enthralling and worth revisiting, are physical representations of their owners' personalities.

When I began hunting special garages, I owned a three-car garage and a 10-car pole barn, both on a 112-year-old farm. They were slowly decaying homes to more birds and chipmunks than cars, although at one time the pole barn held a Miata, a replica Porsche Spyder, two BMW 2002s, a monster Lincoln coupe, an Italian sport bike, a Triumph dirt racer, and a racing go kart. Since then I've built a new three-car garage that's coincidentally attached to a new house, and I plan to do all the stuff to it that I've learned from the car people in this book.

Bruce Massman's garage comes complete with a plug-in stoplight. **Bill Delaney**

Some of the improvements include adding epoxy paint on the floor, a lift, more electrical outlets than I can count, compressed air plumbing, and other necessities of car lust. I know I'll miss the rough-hewn walnut timbers that made an excellent engine hoist in the old barns. Smaller places like my newly constructed three-car garage tend not to collect the variety of interesting machines that a big space allows. And wherever you have special vehicles, like-minded enthusiasts gather. So I'm keeping a book filled with sketches and I'm keeping an eye out for my ultimate garage.

—Phil Berg

Part 1

The Garage as a Palace

1

Candy Store

A Clubhouse for Cars

No secret handshake is required, but this garage is for members only

For two decades, 35 special cars from the collections of 35 serious car guys have been parked in a restored 1928 Packard dealership. The brick-and-timber building lies within the sight of many people who would be curious and eager to see this near-mythical place. Yet there is no publicity, nothing that would give away the urban location of this carefully redecorated palace for cars.

This is a secret place.

It's called the Candy Store, a name given to it by its founders, Russell Head and Robert Cole, two well-known car collectors and dedicated enthusiasts. Bob Cole, a former race car driver, ran a Jaguar dealership in the area, and Russ Head was active in concours until he passed away in 1985. Cole, who remains active in the club, just won the Candy Store's "Esprit de Club" award for organizing events and cars on display.

The Candy Store name is actually carried over from another building leased by the founders in the late 1970s. The lease expired, and members who had their cars stored there found themselves garageless.

When the Packard dealership became available nearby, the members restored it and in 1983 moved in, throwing a glamorous white-tie party to celebrate. Other top-secret clubhouses like this exist around the country, trying to preserve the anonymity of their members and their locations. However, few museums have rarer and more spectacular car collections than the Candy Store.

Section opener: Stanley Gold designed his garage to hold 15 of his favorite Porsches. Phil Berg

Previous page: Beyond the Alfa 6C are the steps to the offices of the Candy Store. Curtains prevent casual glances from people on the sidewalk just beyond the large windows. George Olson

"We don't allow people to wander in," says Joe Brilando, former president and activity chairman. The building has an elaborate alarm system, but the monetary value of the cars is not the primary concern. It's that some of the cars are irreplaceable, one-of-a-kind, and original models.

Beyond the hood ornament of the 1937 Mercedes 540K, near the front picture windows of the Candy Store, is a 1952 Bentley Type R. George Olson

The windows upstairs are part of the office space that looks out over a Ferrari 375 America Vignale and a 1962 250GT Spyder. George Olson

A glance at the roster of the current collection of 35 cars in 2003 included rare machines such as a 1934 ERA, a 1906 Locomobile, a 1953 Ferrari 375 America Vignale that was a featured star of the Paris auto show that year, and a 1926 Bugatti T39A. Clean examples of rare American cars also are parked under the Candy Store's big wooden ceiling, including a Chrysler 300 recently borrowed by Chrysler itself for a car show. All the cars are privately owned, and the rules of the place require that they be driven on a regular basis.

Since 1983, when the current Candy Store building was opened, Cole says that the cars a member has brought inside have been as important for membership as who the member was that brought them.

Organized with 35 regular members and 25 associate members, the club allows regular members to park one car each in the Candy Store. Associates join in for dinners, parties, monthly speeches, and organized drives on weekends. Guests are frequently invited for the monthly gatherings.

"To become a member, you need three members to recommend you, plus a car of distinction," says Brilando. The entire group votes on a candidate, and the seven-member board of directors decides what distinction means. The club also has a car committee, which determines where in the large building members can

A small wet bar is tucked underneath the office space and opens onto the main floor.
George Olson

An antique fuel pump stands at the bar's entrance. Behind it are photos of the guest speakers who have come to the club. George Olson

park their cars. The building is divided into two sections for cars: the front "showroom," with large, two-story glass windows, and the rear "service" area. Brilando says the front is reserved for the most unique cars.

"We're right at capacity now. A new member can be voted in only when somebody quits. Right now, there are people on the waiting list," Brilando adds. The size of the club is limited by the amount of space in the

building. But, the club has found that its small size allows members to get to know each other well.

In 1983, the core club members—who included known car collectors Jules Heumann, Herb Boyer, Sid Colberg, and Lorin Tryon, among others—hired crews to sandblast the old paint from the wooden beams and pour a new cement floor. Other than that, the original members did the restoration themselves. They built a kitchen and they restored and installed a bar, which came surplus from a passenger steamship. Member Heumann, who was in the furniture business, donated much of the furniture.

A major earthquake in 1987 prompted the club to retrofit the building to make it stronger, though it didn't sustain irreparable damage and all the cars survived. Steel girders now augment the arched wooden roof with engineered tie bars, all painted to match the color of the wood.

Daylight comes from the sky windows that were installed by the members during the restoration. The walls display signs and memorabilia belonging to the them, and a photo wall near the bar exhibits photos of current and former members and guests.

Despite being housed here, cars are not worked on in the Candy Store. "It's like a yacht club," says Brilando. "You bring your car in, take it out, and if you have to work on it, take it somewhere else. They have to be running and used. They have to be taken out and driven. That's the rules."

On Saturday mornings, you can find open hoods and the electrical outlets on the outside walls in use for battery chargers so that the cars can be started quickly. "That's what separates a garage from a museum," explains Brilando. Even the Locomobile and the other pre-1920s classics are runners.

"Some members take great pride in doing their own work on their cars, but local regulations prohibit the building from being used as a workshop," says Brilando.

The original wooden beams inside the former auto dealership were reinforced to meet California's strict earthquake codes.
George Olson

The original Candy Store building had a full restoration shop in it. But one of the drawbacks of having a working shop is that thick dust from extensive bodywork would settle on the finished cars.

On special "second Tuesdays," formal gatherings are held at the Candy Store. Additional gatherings are scheduled during the winter, when collectors typically have their cars in restoration shops and are not out driving them. Also, a select group of organizations are permitted to hold dinners. "We mostly limit it to the car world, like Mercedes or Maserati. We have a Ferrari event every year," says Brilando. "We had a great vintage motorcycle event with Vincents and Nortons."

Speakers have included former Grand Prix drivers Phil Hill, Carroll Shelby, and Dan Gurney, as well as famous collectors and concours show winners. Local dignitaries

The 1988 Williams FW12 is one of a few cars not driven regularly on the street. George Olson

have also spoken and often attend the monthly speeches and gatherings.

Personal functions are also held in the Candy Store. "My 50th birthday party was the most memorable, because it was there," says Brilando, who joined the club in 1986. "Many of the members were there. There are

A 427 Cobra parked at the far end of the main floor is still visible from the large office windows over the library. George Olson

family events—we've had wedding receptions and anniversaries, and a lot of birthday parties."

Colossal showroom windows in the front of the building are covered by thin curtains, which prevent the public from discovering the fabulous cars parked inside. A second floor, above the library and bar that separate

the showroom from the service area, includes the original business offices of the Packard dealership. Some of the members use these offices, so the building is occupied most of the day.

Flanking the single large garage door where the cars enter and exit is the large kitchen, closed off by

In front of these posters decorating the library walls, banquet tables can be set up to serve dinners. The Candy Store has a full kitchen flanking the single garage door by which cars enter. George Olson

curtains, but no workbenches or toolboxes are hidden anywhere. When the club first moved into this building, the board members were known as the "kitchen cabinet," because this is where they held meetings.

On a typical Saturday morning with pleasant weather, members come by, start up their cars, and take them for drives in the country. But you won't find a detailed description of their routes here, lest it compromise the Candy Store's location.

You can look for a simple slogan, however, used on official communiqués by members: "Great cars, great people."

2

Stanley Gold

Pride of Porsches

This dream garage
is dedicated to just
one famous marque

Thirteen years ago, Stanley Gold got back at his mother.

"I came home from high school one day and said I wanted to take auto mechanics. My mother went ballistic. She said, 'You have to go to college; you have to take advanced placement classes.' I told her I will go to college, but I just want to learn about cars. So she wouldn't let me take the auto mechanics class."

Gold went to college, started a family, and became a highly successful businessman. Then, while jogging on

Previous page: In the six years since Stanley Gold built his dream garage, he's adorned the walls with photos and posters of his Porsche adventures. **Phil Berg**

the beach in Malibu in 1990, the shape of a Porsche 356 under a car cover made the 44-year-old Gold stop.

"I was too embarrassed to ask about the car, but my friend who was jogging with me knocked on the door and asked if the car was for sale," he recalls. "And the

The special black tile for the garage came from Italy. Gold credits his wife for much of the garage's design. **Phil Berg**

To avoid having to install a lift to work on his cars, Gold built an underground pit in the back corner of the garage. The pit also doubles as golf club storage. Phil Berg

A full kitchen with humidor and wine cellar supports gatherings of Porsche and other car enthusiasts. In a pinch, the area can be used as a workshop. Phil Berg

guy's wife, who answered the door, shouted, 'Yes, it's for sale.' " The car was a mundane 1964 red coupe, but Gold spent a year and a half having it restored to concours quality.

In the next 12 years, Gold acquired a museum-level collection of more than a dozen special Porsches. In that time he's competed with them in tours and races, culminating in 2002 when one of his cars won the first Petit Le Mans, a vintage endurance race. In his garage, Gold has a 911 Porsche police car, a rare Swiss four-seat roadster with a 911 driveline, and an equally rare Abarth

The rare 959 is flanked by some of Gold's favorites, yet he's still looking for another 550 Spyder and another Abarth Carrera. Phil Berg

The upstairs lounge, illuminated by three large sky windows, is filled with books and magazines about Porsches. The large wooden ceiling beams were inspired by a similar design in Gold's office. **Phil Berg**

Speedster, as well as special edition 911s and a Boxster.

"So this is really getting back after 40 years," Gold says.

The collection wasn't enough, however. Six years ago, he moved from a moderately sized Beverly Hills house to a much bigger place, just to be able to build the garage of his dreams.

"I lived four houses down the street from this house. My neighbor was walking his dog one night and I told him I had a new car to show him," recalls Gold. "He came and looked and said it was a beautiful car, but the garage was junk. It was an old prewar garage. Homeless people used to sleep in it."

Gold told his wife that he'd like to get an architect and build a proper garage to house his growing Porsche collection. His wife wanted to add a game room to the side of the garage, and eventually it became clear to Gold that he didn't have enough property. Then his current house came on the market. It had a much bigger yard in back—enough for an ultimate garage—so the Golds moved.

"I came out one summer day and they had dug the foundation. I had a glass of wine in my hand and was sort of overlooking my empire here," Gold remembers, telling his wife that he could fit 10 cars into the new garage. His wife answered that she could get 75 for dinner in the new garage, if the cars were moved onto the lawn. "She told me, 'There's a full kitchen in it, there's a bathroom in it. We'll have parties out here.' "

An architect drew the basic layout. "I like open wood beams," says Gold. But the architect had added some beams the Golds didn't like. "So then everybody, from the contractor to my wife, changed it," recalls Gold. "The floor is very big, expensive Italian ceramic tiles. The guys started laying them, and they didn't match. There was an odd batch. So my wife told the workers the tiles didn't match. They said, 'This is a garage, lady.' She said we paid for matching tile, and they pulled up the tiles and put them back."

"I wasn't sure the architect did a great job—a lot of it was my wife," he explains. "We wanted the apron to match the house, so it ended up being all brick." The garage occupies a space that used to be two tennis courts. "I didn't have any problems meeting code, and I did not want any windows to the alley because I didn't want people busting in or looking in, so we backed it all up against a solid surface."

"We didn't want lifts because this is a big rumpus room," adds Gold. So to allow access for working on the cars, Gold designed a basement room with a grease pit opening to the display floor.

"We needed the neighbors to sign off—the pit is a nonconforming use because it's underground. So our neighbors would come by to look at this pit under construction because they had to sign off on it. One guy asked, 'What are you doing? Building a bomb shelter?' Another one asked, 'What are you making, a ritual bath tub?' And I'd say, 'Stop it. This is a pit to change oil.' "

The kitchen, under the loft lounge and office, lines the alley side of the garage. Next to it is a wine cellar, a cigar humidor, and a cache of champagne magnums. A staircase in back leads down to the oil-change pit, which is full of cases of oil and tools.

"I personally don't do anything," Gold admits, proving he hasn't gotten back at his mother completely. "There's a full toolbox, so that you can do any work. I have guys

A small, second-floor office is actually a bridge over a narrow driveway to the caretaker's house. Extra help is a must when there are 10 cars and only three doors. **Phil Berg**

come in and do it." Not many working garages have the attraction of this much champagne on hand.

"This went from nothing to here in six years. I had two or three cars in an old garage here, and I kept a couple in a garage in Malibu, but the salt air is not great for them. I had a mechanic too, and he always had a couple of my cars in somebody else's garage," he recalls.

Gold also has central air conditioning in the garage, which can hold up to 15 cars. "For years we never had air in our house down the street," he says. "Finally I put air in

Gold's extensive model collection is almost entirely Porsche-based and takes up two walls of the first floor.
Phil Berg

the top floors, and when I built the garage, my wife asked, 'What are all those ducts for? You mean the cars get air conditioning and I went for all those years without it?' "

Gold had an interest in Porsches before his obsession took off. "When I first was married, we had a 1972 Porsche, but the kids started getting bigger. So we had a Mercedes, or station wagons, and when I finally got back to sports cars, the kids were off to college. In 1989, I bought a Porsche 911 Carrera. I was interested enough [that] I actually read all the manuals and signed up for the Porsche club."

Gold began to go to tours and races put on by the clubs. "I quickly learned that the people having the most fun were the 356 guys. I had a brand new Porsche, and I thought, 'By gosh, it would be fun to see if I could redo an old car.' " That's when Gold had his fateful jog in Malibu, which resulted in his purchasing a 356.

"I found out it was a nice 356, but there were more desirable cars. There were Speedsters and Carreras, and so for about 10 years, I entered all kinds of cars in concours shows."

By 1998, other members urged Gold to channel his enthusiasm into vintage racing. Gold raced in events all over California. "I started off slowly, in tours and rallies, and last December we were [driving] at 150 miles per hour down the Mulsanne Straight in a 1964 904."

He entered the rare 904 racer in the Petit Le Mans event, alternating driving duties with his partners. "Cars were going by me and I was going by them, and it was the best thing I could ever do. And that's what this whole thing has evolved into."

Gold's 904 came over the finish line second, and the team got a small trophy for that placing, but that was only the team's "raw" score. When corrected scores were tallied, Gold's 904 finished first. The big trophy is in one of several large display cases in the garage, and the 904 sits over the grease pit. The car was an ex-factory racer that once competed in the Le Mans race, the Targa

This diorama in the model collection shows a Porsche garage with wooden beams. **Phil Berg**

Florio in Italy, and the Monte Carlo rally in the 1970s.

Gold has a 1967 Carrera II at a garage in Paris that he has been driving in tours in Europe, but he's made a space for it in the garage. "I will probably bring it home at the end of this season and refresh the motor. I thought I'd run it until the wheels fall off and then bring it home."

Across the alley, one of Gold's neighbors has a small-scale steam railroad around his yard. Gold is dreaming of getting his own railroad in his backyard and a movable track that would attach to his neighbor's track.

"When I want to use it, it would attach to his, and I would run the railroad cars back and forth," he says. Stanley Gold is an example of what can happen when car enthusiasm grabs hold like an obsession.

3

Walter Hill

It Started with One Car

The sweet lines
of Jaguars fill
this motor house

"I just can't throw anything away," says Walter Hill, whose stunning collection of historical Jaguars makes his garage a small museum. Yet it's his respite and a place where he can pursue his self-proclaimed hobby of tinkering. He also keeps the cars running so that he can drive them on his kilometer-long private test track, built next to his garage on an airfield in Florida.

Hill's garage is a modest-looking building that he put up after he retired from a 35-year career as an Eastern Airlines captain and test pilot. From the outside it looks plain, but inside it is a large, clean area, painted bright

THEIR SWEET LINES ALL BUT TAKE MY BREATH AWAY, AND I DESIRE THEM AS MUCH FOR THEIR BEAUTY AS FOR THEIR USE.

It bothers Walter Hill that he hasn't discovered the origin of this saying, which captures his feelings for Jaguars. **Michael Stewart**

white and decorated with memorabilia. His tools and spare parts are crammed into an adjacent hangar, in a corner workshop where he fixes and maintains his cars.

Above the door to his garage, painted in foot-tall letters on a beam, is a saying: "Their sweet lines all but take my breath away, and I desire them as much for their beauty as for their use." Says Hill, "I think that's the most important thing in the building. I'm distressed that I can't remember who said that. It wasn't me. It's like me."

Hill's passion for Jaguars started in 1956. As a test pilot for Eastern, he was on call 24 hours, seven days a week. "I had to make a lot of drives to the airport, and I thought I should get a fun car." Hill's first fun car was an XK140, a faster, more refined version of the XK120 that

Visitors and friends can assemble in the foyer for a tour of Hill's collection. **Michael Stewart**

The garage is one large room with Hill's workbench in an adjacent airplane hangar. **Michael Stewart**

got him interested in racetrack driving and club racing in the late 1950s.

"I took it to many events and got to know about racing people and racing events. It was primarily for transportation. I remember one race at Sebring when it started to overheat and I dropped out. People criticized me for that, and I said, 'Wait, I can't burn this up—I have to go to work tomorrow.' It was a real car."

Hill sold the XK140 shortly after he bought it and almost got out of the Jaguar habit. "My son got old enough that we were fishing. I needed a station wagon,

so I sold the XK140 and bought a wagon. I didn't have enough sense. I wish I still had it."

But other cars caught his eye, and the Jaguar passion returned. "I would be attracted to a car because I knew about the model and wanted to learn about it. Or I saw it advertised and I would fix it up, maybe [do] a full restoration, and I'd race it a few times. But being a pack rat, I never disposed of any of them."

Several non-Jaguars caught Hill's eye, too, and in his garage you'll find a 1933 two-seater Indy car decorated with painted-on polka dots from sponsor Wonder Bread's

Memorabilia and trophies from Hill's racing exploits fill display cases behind these sleek specimens.
Michael Stewart

logo. In fact, you'll find 25 cars in Hill's garage at the airfield. "It's what my English friends call the 'motor house.'" He also has two airplanes in a separate hangar, which also contains his workbench and tools.

Two of the cars Hill considers the most important are a black prewar SS90 and a bronze-colored XK120. "That little black open two-seater was the first competition car that was produced when the company was operating as SS Cars. After the war, they called themselves Jaguar."

Even though Hill only occasionally gives tours of his garage, he's eager to tell the stories behind the cars. He says the rare SS90 was created in 1935 to get some attention for the start-up car company, an outgrowth of Swallow Sidecar Company. Hill considers it the ancestor of all of the racing cars Jaguar would later build. "They only made 23 SS90s, by which time founder William Lyons considered it not up to what he wanted. So the cylinder head was changed to overhead valves from side valves."

The new car was the SS100, of which several hundred were built. "The SS90 was very limited production and didn't accomplish a great deal, but it started the factory thinking about racing. After the war, in the mid-1950s,

This XJ-13 replica sits alongside the other Jaguars in Hill's garage. **Michael Stewart**

they truly dominated in endurance racing with the D-types and C-types and a limited number of lightweight E-types. I think that's important," Hill says.

Hill's next favorite is the bronze XK120—the first production prototype of the series. It spent most of its early life in the factory in Coventry, England. A second prototype was built for testing and speed runs. "In 1948, the factory in great haste put together the XK120 to showcase the engine. They had this double-overhead cam, six-cylinder XK engine—it was a copy of the racing

engine. They showed the car at a motor show in Earl's Court, and people went bonkers over the car. So Jaguar founder William Lyons said, 'I'll have to make some more of them.' "

In 1949, a new class of production-based racing car convinced Jaguar to enter the XK120 in a race at the famed Silverstone track in England. The company was concerned, however, that the car was "too big and too heavy. . . . So they took those two cars out at night and concluded they could be competitive." The car Hill now

Rare Jaguar racers sparked Hill's collecting bug. Michael Stewart

owns finished the Silverstone race in second place, while another XK120 won the race.

Another race at Palm Beach Shores attracted the Jaguars, and Hill's car was painted red for legend Briggs Cunningham to enter with his team of special race cars. It finished third, behind an Indy car and a Cunningham special. "When I found out the car was in the U.S., I thought I'd get it," recalls Hill, who bought the car in the 1970s.

The pattern of buying one-of-a-kind racing Jaguars continued throughout Hill's life: "If there's a theme in what I've done, it's that I have a car that represents the earliest specification of every model, and a second car, at least one, that is the highest specification that the model was ever taken to. It doesn't prove a damn thing, but you can

see the 1961 E-type with serial No. 27, and then the 1974 E-type with the 12-cylinder in home market form." Those are the first and last years the famed XK-E was produced.

When Hill bought the right hand–drive 1974 E-type, he had to declare to the U.S. Department of Transportation that he was importing the car only for display. "After five years on display, the government will let you drive it on the road. If you're stopped before then, it will be confiscated and will cost you three times the value of the car." Hill solved the problem of driving this nonfederalized car by building his own test track around the airfield on his property.

Hill was thrilled when vintage racing gained popularity in the 1970s, but he thinks these days it's far removed from its roots. "We were doing then what we

This 1933 Indy race car at center was sponsored by Wonder Bread, which explains the polka dot design. Michael Stewart

should be doing now but aren't. We would take a standard car and go out and have a good time. You dice with your friends on the track and stay out of a stranger's wreck. I did a lot of that."

At 83, Hill is thinking about what might happen to his collection in the future, but he may follow a model of finding good homes for the cars set years ago by a former service manager for a Jaguar dealer in Rhode

The garage is modest looking from the outside, belying the collection of rare Jaguars inside. **Michael Stewart**

Island. Legendary importer Max Hoffman bought a Jaguar XK120 in late 1954, when the cars were new, as Hill recalls the story. A dealer in the Northeast sold Hoffman the car, and then after a few races it went to a service manager. "He altered the car over time and did a lot of racing. He never would sell it, but he died and his son was the executor of his estate. I had lunch with the family, and the boys were telling me granddad had the fastest car on the block," Hill says.

The service manager's will stated that the proceeds from the sale of the former Hoffman Jaguar would be held in a trust account for the education of his grandsons. "That brought tears to my eyes," says Hill, who bought the car from the family in the 1970s. "It's a good way to buy a car.

"That XK120 was claimed to be all original, and they never are. I had to buy a parts car that was 95 percent original to return the first car to its original condition. I have another one that's light blue—all of the XK120s were pastel colors. That's my clean car—when I go to club events and shows, that's what I take. I worked hard to get that car right."

"I am a tinkerer and a pack rat," Hill adds. "My activities reflect those two things, tinkering and not being able to dispose of anything. That's what the definition of collector is. People talk to me and ask me about my collection, and I say 'What collection?' They say, 'You're a world-renowned collector,' and I say, 'I don't know how to behave like a collector.' They say, You're doing just fine.' "

4

Jay Leno

Projects Expand to Fit the Space

There's no
bar in here;
this is not
a pool hall

On an average workday, comedian Jay Leno cruises from the Burbank studio where he works to his compound of three enormous airplane hangars that have been converted into garages for his favorite 80 cars and 60 motorcycles. When he arrives in a clean 1949 Hudson slightly after dinnertime, he wanders into the dirtiest of the three buildings, the one with the machine shop and a dozen special projects underway.

Parked near the large door of the building, next to a motorcycle powered by a Bell Ranger helicopter turbine,

Previous page: Jay Leno's passion for cars includes everything from special modern cars to Golden Age classics. **John Lamm**

is a Hummer H2. It's the only vehicle in the garage that doesn't belong to Leno. General Motors loaned it to him on the chance that he will drive it and maybe mention it on his television show. He walks over and peeks inside the H2, notably the most eye-popping and profitable truck for GM in 2002.

One corner of the shop is devoted to motorcycle restoration, but with the number of projects that are underway, parts are scattered everywhere. **Phil Berg**

"Nah, it's not for me," he says, staring for a moment at the thick plastic shifter in the center console. "Too much plastic."

He ignores the H2 and says to Bob Sales, one of five full-time employees at the Leno garage compound, "I'll take the Morgan home."

Leno is the embodiment of hands-on car enthusiasm unchecked by external forces. The 53-year-old comedian is manic, sweating in the 70-degree hangar with his denim shirt unbuttoned almost to his waist. He gazes at the quarter-completed restorations and hot rod conversions with the eye of a factory manager while chewing a thumb-sized ball of gum hard and fast. As he sits on a metal folding chair to hear the progress reports from his crew, his foot taps a rapid staccato on the chipped and stained concrete floor.

Expert steam mechanic John Kelso asks Leno about the engine in a rare Doble steam car. Leno replies, "The problem is [that there is] no way anybody can get a thousand miles on a tank of water. You can't condense that

One of Leno's projects is to set steam-powered records for speed and distance using these rare Doble steam cars. **Phil Berg**

much steam that quickly. The steam temperature usually runs 625 degrees. By the time steam goes through the throttle, through the compound engines, through the high and low cylinders, you're dangerously close to water. We could have gotten a little bit more because of running it at a cooler temperature, but I would rather have the hot steam than cooler water."

Kelso nods in thought. Leno continues, "Second of all, there's tremendous leaks through the wall. And steam coming out of the rear ball union—that's a problem. Then you have that ball union spring—are you going to do that tomorrow?"

Leno is speaking to Kelso in the language of steam power, fast and foreign to the other four employees who have gathered to brief Leno. "I think if we fix those leaks we double the distance straight off the top. If you can get 100 miles off a tank, that's good. Once in a while 200. I don't want to lower the temperature because . . ."

Leno has no particular favorite cars or motorcycles, and new modified Corvettes can be found parked next to antique Bugatti racers. **John Lamm**

The third hangar is the clean display area with about 70 running cars waiting to be driven. It has a small lounge area with seating and coffee tables. John Lamm

He trails off, seeing that Kelso understands.

Of the 40 or so rare Doble steam cars produced in the early 1920s, Leno has two and figures that maybe four or six are still running somewhere in the world. He wants to set a speed and distance record in one. "We can do it because back then they couldn't get enough pressure in the steam tank, but we're using the heat exchanger from a Titan missile. It's amazing what you can find if you hang around an air force junkyard."

He wanders over to an old refrigerator and pulls out a bottle of water. The current project cars sit parked in two rows in the center of the working garage. The walls are lined with lifts on one side, a full machine shop with a chassis dynamometer next to a row of four Stanley Steamers on another side, and a parts room and two Dobles next to the lunch table. Off in the distance is a Jaguar XJ6 stripped to its shell on one of six lifts.

Leno doesn't fit into any standard category of car nut.

He doesn't restore old cars exactly to original specifications, but he keeps them close to the intent of the original producer. He offers his car philosophies freely. "Old cars are just modifications on modifications. The guys who built these things were engineers, and they were built to run a certain way at a specific time. Like the Stanleys. People drove down the roads—well, there weren't any roads, so cars had to bend, or they broke in half." His hands mimic a bending frame. "So the chassis were extremely flexible so they literally would step over bumps. That's why they did it."

The history lesson continues. "People knew about overhead camshafts and all that kind of stuff, but the

The machine shop rivals any large professional shop's capabilities. **Phil Berg**

manufacturing wasn't up to the task. People worked with what they had available at the time. Back then, labor was cheap and technology was expensive. Now it's the other way around."

He's not just ranting about history in general. "On the Bentley motor, you got 280 little bolts holding the water jacket on. Why do you need that? Because it was strong and it didn't cost anything. The guy on the line got 15 cents an hour putting a few bolts on, and it's not the end of the world. Back then, if you wanted technology, it cost you a fortune. Now technology costs nothing, but some of the guys putting on the bolts you gotta pay health insurance, benefits."

His foot continues to tap. He doesn't revere the fascinating workmanship of old cars as much as he loves putting himself in the shoes of their creators, improving on the creations. "I love brass-era cars," he says, beaming with pride at his Franklin. You get the idea he believes he was born in the wrong time period and could easily have been a 1930s auto designer.

Leno prefers to spend his time in the working shop of the main hangar. The race car to his left belongs to a shop employee. **John Lamm**

Giant murals hang in the second of three hangars. This one is populated mainly by Duesenbergs and racing Bentleys. John Lamm

Then again, he looks with the same admiration at the two modern motorcycles next to his Franklin. "Technology is fun," he continues, "That's a jet engine. That's a Wankel. I like projects."

Steam mechanic Kelso has wandered back to the machine shop 200 feet away in another corner of the

hangar. Leno really breaks into a smile when he talks about driving the Doble steam car at 75 miles per hour on the freeway. "I don't really get a chance to do any drives—I'm working all the time. I just go out in a big circle and come back to the garage—sometimes 50 miles, sometimes 250 miles."

Parts storage rooms are built into the corners of the hangars. Their walls are decorated by Leno's own memorabilia, which he has collected over a lifetime of car enthusiasm. John Lamm

The next of Leno's mechanics shows him a six-inch diameter fire-hose connector made of brass. "It'll look better if we paint it silver," he says. Leno is restoring a 1940s vintage fire truck to use as a sag wagon for motorcycles. When finished, it will have a rear deck that hydraulically lowers to the ground so that he can roll a broken motorcycle onto it. One of the two "clean" buildings holds about 60 motorcycles.

More special project cars have pieces of Leno's attention. Next to the fire truck is the 1955 Buick Roadmaster Leno drove to California when he moved there more than two decades ago to expand his show business career. It has a fond place in his heart and, until a few months ago, had been sitting unused in the backyard of his mother-in-law's home.

But he doesn't plan to restore it to the condition it was in when it was his daily driver in the late 1970s—no, he's adding a Z06 Corvette drivetrain with a supercharger for a total output of 650 horsepower. Corvette brakes, suspension, and steering also will be added. He talks about sectioning the wheels so high-performance tires that still look mostly stock can be used.

Leno has no plan to collect cars, but he gets a surplus of offers. "Guys know I like certain cars, and they also know if they sell them to me, I'll keep them forever, keep them running. There's nothing I have my eye on. I wasn't looking for a 1956 Chrysler Imperial, but someone told me they had it, and I saw it was perfect. So I got a great 1956 Chrysler that I enjoy driving."

Seated at the shop's lunch table, which is piled high with old car magazines and copies of *Hemmings Motor News*, Leno listens to his chief mechanic Bernard Juchli give him a rundown on the rest of the projects. Leno

Some 60 motorcycles are kept ready should Leno decide to go riding early on a Sunday morning.
John Lamm

explains that he's here at the garage only for an hour, then he'll drive back to the studio to finish new comedy material with *The Tonight Show* writers. "Saturday I have to go to Vegas to do a Doritos commercial," he tells Juchli, who seems to consider Leno's coming absence a minor nuisance in the overall occupation of building cars.

When asked how many hours he works in a day, Leno responds, "You mean on the *Tonight Show*? Look at all this. I have to pay for it somehow."

The scale of Leno's private collection makes him uneasy when he considers what people might think about him. "If I start telling you how many cars I have, someone might get the idea I'm showing off all this stuff, and this isn't the time to do that—we're in the middle of a recession. Everyone except the car guys always ask, 'How much did all this cost?' 'What's the fastest car you have?' 'Which movie star had one of those?' "

Leno had a nine-car garage at his home in Beverly Hills before he bought the first airplane hangar. He had no plan

Despite the work Leno puts into keeping his cars in top running shape, he says he has no interest in building his own design. John Lamm

to expand it to three hangars. He bought the first hangar because it would hold a lot of cars and the neighbors wouldn't be bothered, no matter how much noise he made.

Then he wanted to buy an adjacent hangar, but it was unavailable. So he built a second building to store his show-quality Duesenbergs, Packards, Stutz, and other restored classics in a tasteful-looking, wooden-beamed museum. Then the adjacent hangar came up for sale, and that's how he wound up with three.

"One thing leads to another, and I added a machine shop, a dyno. It's amazing how many friends come out of the woodwork when you have a dyno."

The gum chewing has slowed, the foot-tapping stopped, and Leno says, "My favorite year in cars was

probably 1932. By '32 they knew how to make cars reliable. It wasn't a problem. That's the year they started making them fast, luxurious, comfortable. They could all afford to hire the best designers in the world because of the Depression. So they all built dream machines."

After an hour at the shop, he walks over to the largest of the three hangars, finds his Morgan in a row of 20 cars, and drives back to the Burbank studio where *The Tonight Show* writers are waiting to work through new material. Then, if this is an average day, he either heads home or to his favorite loop of roads through southern California—sometimes driving 50 miles, sometimes 250 miles.

5

Bruce Massman

A Home for the Antiques

Early retirement
spurred this
brass-era fanatic
to keep his cars
close by

"You don't get up in the morning and then drive somewhere else to get dressed," says Bruce Massman. "It's like waking up and leaving your clothes a mile away." That's why the 57-year-old fan of driving antique cars won't keep any cars unless they're in the garage next to his Beverly Hills home.

The house came with a garage connected by an archway, but now that garage has been turned into an exercise room. **Bill Delaney**

In 1984, he built a five-car, single-story garage behind his home. He thought it would be big enough for all the cars that interested him, but he quickly filled the place. At the time, he had a couple of Packards, an Auburn, and an elegant old Cadillac. After acquiring a rare Lozier, a Stutz, a special Chrysler, and a Duesenberg seven years later, he extended the height of the roof and added a double door in the back of the garage leading to the alley. "I needed some serious space," he recalls.

His expansion plan was for a garage with five doors facing a courtyard and a sixth double door opening into an alley. He wanted a building tall enough to hold five lifts so that he could stack five cars on top of five others. But he didn't want the building to look like a two-story box. "We had to find out what the city would allow us to do. So I said to the architect, 'Short cars over here and long cars over here. You design it how big you think you want, and then make it even bigger.' "

The Ferrari used to be red. Like the Stutz, Massman prefers it in yellow, even though purists are appalled it has not been kept in its original color. Bill Delaney

Originally, the large house had a two-car garage attached, but when he built the first five-car structure, he converted the two-car garage into a game and exercise room. At the same time, he decided to expand his house, stretching one side almost into his neighbor's yard. But the setback rules in Beverly Hills were on the brink of change.

"The architect turned the plans in two days late, after the date the setback ordinance changed. I lost 1,500

Massman had his lifts painted white to blend with the interior of the garage. The lifts are mounted so they can rock—and not break—during an earthquake. **Bill Delaney**

square feet on the house." The new rules mean he's likely not going to be able to expand the garage any more, but he figures that's nature's way of telling him 12 cars is enough for his collection.

He's managed to get along just fine with the house and the big garage, although he still raises the eyebrows of his neighbors. "I park my car trailer on the street, and the neighbors go, 'What kind of white trash is living here?' " Massman is a native of Beverly Hills, but adds, "I'm not the right person for the area. I used to drive a motorcycle every morning."

Massman is pleased with the way the finished garage looks inside. "You're not looking at stud walls. Women come in here and they don't mind. My wife tells her friends to come out here; it's not a garage." One side window looks over the pool, and all the windows are dressed with blinds. "When you have friends over, it's amazing—even guys who don't like the cars want to take a photo of the car with the wife and kids, and they say, 'I love that photo, and I put it on my desk.' "

The five lifts in Massman's garage share posts and are bolted to the floor through slotted holes so that the whole structure will rock but not fall down during an earthquake. The famous Northridge quake in California knocked over a Honda of Massman's, which then scratched the Aston Martin parked next to it, but not one of the cars on the lifts was harmed.

When you glance inside Massman's garage, it looks a bit crowded with 12 cars and only five doors. But there is enough room to open doors without banging adjacent cars.

"Let's say I'm working on a car. I need my electrical outlets everywhere. They're all built flush. The only thing I didn't really do as well is plumb for an air compressor, but I use a portable with a 150 pounds pressure, which is more than I need," he explains. The floor sits lower than the alley, and a cement ramp leads from the back of the garage to the alley. Massman put in a drain to catch water, but it flooded once during an uncharacteristically heavy rainstorm. "We don't get a ton of rain every year, but when we do it's a shock to the city."

Because he is a fan of so-called "brass" cars, automobiles that are built with brass trim, Massman has tailored his garage to their particular needs. "Right now, I have diamond-plate decking under each car for the floor. Brass cars notoriously leak; otherwise they're not brass," Massman explains. "You really have to pay attention to ventilation. All the old cars smell a certain way because they leak. You can't get the gas smell out, so you have to make sure you ventilate."

Massman started collecting brass cars after a trip to

Massman told his architect to add several feet to the dimensions of his garage so that long touring cars like this Cadillac would fit inside. **Bill Delaney**

Hershey, Pennsylvania, where he visited the famed swap meet there. He says he always liked sports cars as a youth but had no interest in historical cars. "I was reading the paper one day, and it has a 1930 Buick roadster in it for sale. So I called up and started to negotiate a price, but the guy wouldn't go any lower because he needed the money for a house. So I said, 'I'll send you a check, and you send me a car.'

"I got the car. It was unrestored—it was a wreck. I drove it for years and never had a problem. It was my first classic. Then I went to Hershey and bought a Packard and another Packard. Then it started eating on me, and I bought this Cadillac and this Auburn and everything else. To me, there is nothing like going down a road in a brass car," he says. "It's a great way to see the country. You get to see things you never see because people invite you in when you're in the old cars—they open up things they don't usually open up to people.

"When I started getting the brass cars, my neighbor said, 'You know, what is it with you? The older the car, the bigger the smile.' For some reason, I didn't get hooked on hot rods. Maybe I'll want something that will be more dependable than the brass cars, but there's some charm about them. We did a sports car rally once, and I took the Marmon. There was a Ferrari section, an Alfa section, a Corvette section, a Porsche section, and I asked them, 'Where's the Marmon section?'

"I tour with everything. I take this Packard out for lunch or for 600 to 1,000 miles for a tour. After a long run in a brass car, you find that the doors don't close the same. Driving them is a whole different thrill. What I like about the brass cars so much is you get to view the area more. In the Ferrari, you're going 140 per hour sometimes, and you can't look at anything."

The Honda, normally parked in the workshop area, was the only vehicle damaged in the last earthquake—it fell over. **Bill Delaney**

This compact work area is functional and decorated with posters from the historical racing era. **Bill Delaney**

One of Massman's favorite stories involves driving his Stutz on the freeway during a tour. On a downhill exit ramp, the brakes glazed over. "If you hit the brakes too hard on a brass car, you'll glaze them immediately. Then you lose them," he explains. His Stutz was headed for an intersection, and even retarding the timing didn't seem to slow the car any. When he got to the intersection, the light was red. But he was able to make a sharp left and

The requisite antique gas pumps stand by the gate to the pool. Massman's house is on the left and the garage is on the right. **Bill Delaney**

60

The sliding rear door opens into the alley. From the inside, it looks like a wall instead of a door. **Bill Delaney**

avoid any traffic. He reached for the horn, but it didn't work. Since then, he's made a point of collecting the biggest bulb horns he can find at swap meets.

"On a brass car drive, everybody is dependent on everybody else. There's a different camaraderie. The guy next to you is the guy who's going to be helping you. The sports cars, they usually don't break down that much," he says. "You have to do your own servicing on a brass car drive, check your own oil, and walk around the car to see what came loose from vibrations.

"I really enjoy these cars. I just have the thrill of driving that era of car. If a car has that look that gets your blood going, that's the car for you. I knew a guy who had a Duesenberg. I asked if he ever drove it, and he said, 'Oh, no it's a Duesenberg.' In the Lozier, it's the only one of its kind. Nobody can believe I drive it. It's an expensive car, and I'd hate to have it hit, but that's what it's made for. It was built in 1908, and it will cruise at 70 miles per hour. You have only so many driving days."

6

Bruce Meyer

Meet Mister Garage

When toy companies
come calling, you know
you've got it good

Bruce Meyer is a man eager to share. He let a Mattel make a miniature copy of his 13-car garage to use as the packaging for a set of expensive toy versions of four of America's most famous cars, which Meyer owns. Every confirmed car nut in the country knows about this garage, not because of its size or what's in it, but likely because someone they know has spent time browsing here.

Previous page: The original two-car garage still serves as the entry to the entire building. It contains most of the memorabilia and photos from a life of unchecked car enthusiasm. Bruce Meyer is proudest of his famous Pierson Brothers coupe, which he sends to car shows and museums for display. Dennis Adler

The thick foliage around Meyer's backyard makes it hard to see that the garage holds 13 cars. Phil Berg

It started as a modest California two-car structure behind a charming, extra-spacious 1920s bungalow on a palm-lined drive. Then it grew. "The previous owner stretched it to a four-car garage in 1975," Meyer recalls. "He put an apartment on top of it, too." To fit another car inside, Meyer stretched out another space behind the four-car garage in 1981, when he and his family moved to the location. Seven years later, this fifth single-car space became a corridor to a large, steel-beam-supported eight-car structure with a row of sky windows in a peaked ceiling.

Now it's a focal point for a guy who was raised in California's golden age of car frenzy and who started a couple of the most influential car-culture organizations in the country. This doesn't happen overnight. Like the pervasive collection of memorabilia that fills the walls of Meyer's

Meyer's collection is extensive enough that he has to store some of it away from his home garage. **Phil Berg**

garage, it doesn't happen according to a plan, either.

"I keep about 12 or 13 cars here. The space would be a problem if I had a lot of big cars," Meyer explains, "but I like little cars." He has a couple of big cars, however, including a Duesenberg, a Mercedes convertible that Clark Gable used to tool around in, and a Packard. "I love the Clark Gable car for driving around town because it's pretty comfy."

The garage has only two double-size doors, one leading to a driveway to the street and one leading to the alley behind the house. Inside the original part of the garage in front, the cars are parked close to old photos on the walls, and with the antique gas pump nearby, the area has the cozy character of a classic garage. Step through the short hall to the new building in the rear and you arrive in a modern garage with a high ceiling. Large windows in the walls and ceiling combine to let light flood in and illuminate the cars.

"I move the cars around a lot," he explains. "Every Friday, I take a car and drive it about a hundred miles. There's always something here that I can drive. The most fun I've had is in the last car I've had out. They're like children—none are better than the others."

In the past week, Meyer has driven his black Gull Wing Mercedes and his chopped 1932 hot rod. "I think the hot rod is the purest automotive art form to come out of the U.S. Baseball, jazz, and hot rods are pure American."

A clean Porsche 356 coupe sits next to a dark blue Cobra. "I just drove this Porsche 870 miles last weekend. It rained the whole time, and the Porsche is good in the rain." Every weekend, in addition to his Friday drives, he takes some kind of drive in one of his cars, and about three times a year he tries to do a California Mille–style long-distance rally. "The driving for me now is the major force in my life."

Meyer's collection isn't limited to hot rods and European sports cars. "I have a Top Fuel dragster that was Don Prudhomme's first car," he says. "From drag-

sters to Duesenbergs, I just love 'em all. That 550 Maranello is pretty new, and that's about the nicest car I've had. Bobby Rahal has one, and we both agree that's about the best-driving new car we've ever had. My wife has an E55, but I drive a Suburban every day."

He owns a few more cars than will fit in the garage, including the famous Pierson Brothers coupe. He keeps some of his cars on display at the Petersen Museum in Los Angeles. "I have a little warehouse in town and the Petersen. The Duesenberg is getting a little paint work on it, so it's at the restoration shop."

Meyer's friendly and diplomatic manner helped him convince the established car collectors at the famed Pebble Beach concours show to allow his beloved hot rods on the display lawn. "For years I tried to get Pebble to accept hot rods. I lobbied the guys in charge. Every time a famous hot rod was restored, I sent them copies of photos and articles about them. I think it's an important part of our heritage."

In 1997, the Pebble Beach board allowed a one-time historic class that included hot rods, usually the 1932 Ford coupe and convertible-bodied flathead V-8–powered cars. Then again in 2002, hot rods found their way among the world's top classic cars at Pebble Beach, largely because of Meyer's efforts.

Meyer can't remember not loving cars. "My mother had this baby book, and my mother wrote in the column, 'Bruce loves anything with wheels.' " His parents bought him a lawnmower engine when he was 12, which he promptly installed onto his wagon. He moved on to build a dune buggy, and he built a Whizzer—a bicycle with a tiny engine. "Motorcycles were always a real important part of my youth, but they had to stay under cover," he confesses. "My parents hated motorcycles."

"I bought my first collector car in 1963—it was the Gull Wing Mercedes. I actually used it as a daily driver. I've had a Gull Wing since 1963, and in 1970 I bought that Ferrari. I've kept it for 33 years. Then I bought that

His broad car and motorcycle passions range from new to old and from sports to luxury cars. Phil Berg

Packard Phaeton that I just sold recently. I'm not much of a seller. I could fill two garages with crap, you know. I just love 'em all, cars and motorcycles. I've had a Cobra since 1965."

Meyer is clear about what a real car nut is. "The car gene is certainly not genetic. My parents hated cars.

When hot rod magazines would come, they'd throw them away if they got to them before I did." He wasn't deterred. "I've got people who come to me and say, 'Help me out, I want to buy a car.' You can't teach a person like that to be a car person. Just buy what you like—that's what it's all about. I'm blessed, though. If

Sky windows illuminate the interior of the rear building, which is connected to the five-car structure in front by a single door. White floor tile extends from the original structure in front to the steel beam-supported building in the rear. Dennis Adler

somebody had told me when I was younger that I would have two Corvettes one day, I wouldn't have believed him. A 1940 Ford was my high school dream car—that's all I wanted."

His latest project is the first Corvette to race at Le Mans. "It's a fun piece. It was restored in 1981, and I kind of redid it again. I raced it at Goodwood [England] two years ago."

His next plan is to drive the California Classic tour in the summer. "I'll take the Gull Wing. My wife will go on that. She enjoys this and the people. I've taken the Pierson coupe to Goodwood, and I run the re-creation of the Tour de France and the Mille Miglia. I'm working on a 1957 Testa Rossa. As soon as I get it done, we'll show it at Pebble. Then I want to just start driving it."

Meyer is chairman of the Petersen Museum, a shrine to automobile nuts, and he's president of a foundation in California called the "11-99" club, which gives scholarships and benefits to the families of California Highway Patrol troopers. The club is not an idle one: This year it awarded $1 million in scholarships to troopers' kids. He's in his local Rotary Club, is an advisor for the Pebble Beach concours, and is on the board of the Nethercutt Collection.

He does have a day job. "I do a fair amount of real estate development, as much time as I can give it. My life is all about the automobile and helping others. I'm on the board of St. John's Hospital. The cars are important, but the community and giving back are, too."

Amid the photos on his walls of famous hot-rodders, racers, and one-of-a-kind moments in racing history, Meyer describes his favorite cartoon: "There's a wonderful cartoon in the *New Yorker*—this guy is on his deathbed in the hospital. His wife is holding his hand, he looks 90 years old, and he looks over at his wife and says, 'I should have bought more crap.' " Meyer acknowledges that the apartment over the original part of his garage is crammed full of auto parts and memorabilia.

The rear section of Meyer's garage is hidden in the trees next to his pool. A double-car door allows entry from the alley. Phil Berg

Does this fantastic garage really provide happiness? "I really am not looking for anything more at this point in my life," Meyer answers. "When I go to car meets and auctions, I'm happier not to find something I want. I've so exceeded my expectations of car ownership that it's a relief to find nothing. To me, the hobby is not owning cars—it's about the people. It's just a fun-spirited group of people to share experiences and loves with. I love talking to the Cobra people, the antique motorcycle people, and the Bugatti guys. If you have a passion for something, that's what it's all about."

"I love it out here in the garage," Meyer says. "Last night, I took a friend from Hong Kong out to dinner, and we got back about 10:30, and I was out here until 11:30. I turn the music on, turn a car on—I could be out here all night. I just love it."

7

Peter Mullin

Blending Art and Cars

A beloved herb
garden forced
this elegant haven
underground

As an art major at UCLA in the early 1960s, Peter Mullin gained an appreciation for sculpture. About 20 years ago, he saw a 1948 Delahaye, a sensuous green machine that the *Los Angeles Times* once labeled the most beautiful car in California. Now Mullin owns about 30 stunning cars, almost all of them show winners and classics from pre- and postwar France. The one common thread that connects all his cars is that they are a unique combination of beauty and function from a narrow period of classic elegance. The journey to becoming an extraordinary car collector focused his perfectionism so finely that in 1990 he built a large Art Deco garage 15 feet underneath his prized herb garden in Los Angeles.

Mullin doesn't just have a moderate affection for these cars—he's more than obsessed. "The difference between art and these automobiles is that the automobiles have a true utility, and art is just something you look at," he says. "There is some speculation why men are drawn to gorgeous cars. The bodies of these cars are almost sinfully designed. Those are nature's curves. The shapes provoke a visceral reaction."

His garage required a painstaking two-year construction. It was designed to blend the style of his 1924 Napoleonic southern colonial home with the deco elegance of the Bugattis, Hispano-Suizas, and Delahayes he keeps inside. It's been featured on television shows, which have called the contents of his garage "the finest collection of French cars in the world," and Mullin is known in classic collectors' circles as an inspiration.

Decorating the walls are large tapestries made of carpet yarns that are individually hand-cut to form images of

A turntable allows Mullin to maneuver more than a dozen cars into his underground garage using only one door. The polished stainless steel turntable platform reflects light under the car. Phil Berg

Opposite page: The garage, larger than allowed by local building codes, was built using a building code exemption available for private museums. Dennis Adler

An electronic "open sesame" signals the door of this vine-covered façade to slide back, revealing the automotive treasures within. Phil Berg

Another of Mullin's famous cars is a 1936 "Teardrop" Talbot-Lago, a show winner and subject of his first cut-yarn tapestry. The faux stone floor of the garage continues up the driveway to the front of the house.
Dennis Adler

Mullin's favorite cars. He commissioned the first tapestry in 1987, and now they fill every available wall panel.

"The garage can carry 15 to 16 cars, depending upon how many you cram in and where," he says. The rest he stores off-site, and some are on display at the Petersen Museum in Los Angeles. "I have some at four or five shops where I have restorations going on," he adds, but admits there's always a problem with space to put his cars.

The architectural vision of the garage proved stressful at times, once he decided to build it in his backyard. "I

Mirrors along one wall make the garage feel larger than its 15-car capacity. **Phil Berg**

love gardens, so I didn't want some 3,000-square-foot block building in my backyard." After thinking about his problem, he decided an underground garage would be the best solution. "It dawned on me that people always build up when they want more space. You add a story to your house. People understand that you own the air above you, but they don't focus on the fact that you own the ground beneath you."

Size was the next hurdle. "The setback rules are horrible," Mullin says. "There was a Los Angeles city code that says a garage can be no bigger than 25 percent of the total square feet of the house. So this house is not big enough to get the size of garage I wanted. I got quite depressed thinking that I needed to get variances and get the neighbors to sign off on them.

"One day my builder called me up and said, 'On page 368 of the L.A. city building code, I found an exception that says a private auto museum is exempt from the 25 percent rule and the setback rules.'" Mullin and his builder decided to call his garage a private auto museum.

The size of the garage was limited by the pool on one side and the lot boundaries on the other sides, but 3,000 square feet of space was left over for the cars, a bar, and two doors disguised as wall panels that lead to a hidden bathroom and wine cellar.

Getting to that design also was a struggle. "I worked with the architect a long time," Mullin recalls. "I kept describing what I wanted, and he kept coming back with what he thought he heard, and it just wasn't working." Finally, at a meeting with the architect, when Mullin was ready to give up the project, the young associate who had been silently attending the meetings announced that he understood what Mullin wanted. "The combination of what was in my head and what was in his skill set in his brain was enough."

Because of the elevation of the property, there was only enough room for one door. The solution to the problem of maneuvering the cars inside the garage was a turntable in the curved doorway. "Backing up this driveway is not fun," says Mullin.

The turntable surface was made with an engine-turned finish. "Like the way you do a Bugatti cam cover," he adds.

Behind the trophy case are couches, a projector, and a movie screen. **Phil Berg**

Behind the Delahaye, hangs a large Bugatti tapestry that is made of raised carpet yarn. The design makes the tapestry appear three dimensional. Phil Berg

An unexpected effect of the shiny spirals on the surface is that as the turntable rotates, the ceiling lights reflect upward into a faux skylight and look like a private light show. "We have functions down here—we use the garage for entertaining—and at night it's quite spectacular."

During daytime, light wells shine down into the garage, and it doesn't feel like it's underground. Mullin was torn between tiling the floor or using stone, but he found a solution on a trip. "I saw a driveway to a great hotel in Atlanta made of pressed concrete, but it looks like there are individual stones. For me it has such a great look, so I just carried it right out all the way up and around the front. It's stained and sealed. It's a perfect display floor—simple, no maintenance—and you can clean up the oil easily."

The garage was born to house the growing collection Mullin was gathering. "It was an interest turned into love, turned into a passion, turned into a disease, probably," he explains. It started with a friend's 1948 Delahaye and a partnership with the friend. "I told him if he ever wanted to own another French car, I'd be interested in doing a joint venture with him for the restoration. Well, we found a car, a 1948 Talbot-Lago, and we restored it together and showed it at the Pebble Beach concours. And we won."

The extraordinary results from Mullin's first classic car fueled his desire for more. "The more you know, the more you love. The more you love, the more you know, and it's a spiral effect," he says. "Prior to that, if you had asked me about French cars, I would have said they were Renault and Citroen. I thought Bugatti was an Italian car. I would have guessed that a Hispano-Suiza was a Spanish and Swiss car. I learned more and more and the thing that really struck me about it was there is a rare combination of high performance, brilliant engineering, and totally sculptural artscape. So if there was ever a definition of rolling sculpture, it would be the prewar French cars."

Currently, Mullin sits on the boards of more than a dozen philanthropic organizations. "I realized that I would never survive as an artist and switched to economics in college," he recalls, "But I had an eye for flowing lines, colors, sculptural mass. What I found is [that] the almost wind-tunnel feel of the great French cars has never been repeated. Most of the new design concepts that come out now, you can probably find some clues in the early French cars."

One of Mullin's favorite cars is the 1937 Delage featured in the movie *An American in Paris*, which he says he loved watching as a kid and still loves to watch today. Leslie Caron drove the car in the movie, but it was owned by Howard Hughes, whose studio produced the film. After the filming, the car sat unused on the back lot of the studio. A Hughes engineer discovered it and traded his retirement account for it. He owned it for 20 years before selling it to Mullin.

Mullin had the car bug before he fell for the French classics. As a sophomore in high school, he and a friend rebuilt a 1953 Chevrolet Belair convertible. "It was painted sienna gold, pinstriped by Von Dutch, and it had 1954 taillights, which was the only difference between the 1953 and 1954 models."

Relying on his friend's mechanical expertise, the two also rebuilt the car's engine. "It smoked when I bought it, which was about 1958. We took it all apart in the driveway at my friend's house rebored the cylinders, reground the valves, and put in new pistons. Amazingly enough, when we put it all together, it ran."

When the two high-schoolers finished their rebuild project, however, a box of parts was left over. "I didn't know where they went, and my friend didn't know, and we thought we marked everything. But the car ran great, so I just put the box in the trunk and drove it for six years," Mullin remembers. When he sold it, he told the next owner if he ever needed the parts, they were in the trunk. "The first car you own certainly kicks you off."

8

David Sydorick

A Place for Centerpiece Cars

A mountainside
was no match for
this Italian car passion

"**W**hat I've always liked is the beauty of the cars, so this garage is a simple space where the cars are the beauties. There's no memorabilia, none of the stuff."

One man's simple space, however, is another's view of a recreated Italian villa, with 1950s and 1960s Italian classic cars. Touring David Sydorick's recently expanded 13-car garage in California takes you into an environment that you might imagine famed designers Zagato and Pinin Farina had planned for their special-bodied Alfa

Romeos, Ferraris, and Maseratis all along. The cars look even better in this fantasy zone than they might winding along the reality of the Mille Miglia route in Italy.

Sydorick believes his garage is merely the frame for the masterpieces. But he doesn't believe in keeping his cars on pedestals: "I drive them all on the street." He built

The rear wall of the main garage under the guesthouse was knocked out for the expansion project. The addition was possible only after the mountainside behind the main garage was excavated. Phil Berg

Before the roof goes on the addition behind the main garage, daylight gives the space the feeling of an open-air pavilion. Phil Berg

his house in 1980 with an attached three-car garage and a second three-car garage that was connected by the trellised archway that leads to his pool. This second three-car garage was under a guesthouse on the hillside lot.

In 1994, he added a single-car space to the three-car section below the guesthouse, careful to blend the stone siding and slate roof so that no one can tell there was an addition. This addition was intended to be the workshop, and it holds all the tools. Even with seven doors and notably tiny cars, he recently ran out of room.

The solution was a major remodeling. "The mountain had to be dug out—the dirt was in the driveway.

The pressed concrete floor is stained green between squares to match the grass sections on the driveway. The floor is eight inches higher at the back wall so that one person easily can roll a car outside before starting it. Phil Berg

The process took six months. Seismic work, permits—it took forever," Sydorick says. "You have to dig pits out there and try to find bedrock, you have to do soil analysis, you have to get approvals from the association, you have to get all that kind of stuff.

"There's a beam underground that runs from here to there—that's a seismic thing. Everything in California is now over-engineered."

"I actually started this project two years, maybe three years before it was finished," he explains. The construction window on mountainsides in California is very narrow, since excavation is not allowed when it might rain and risk a mudslide. The planning also takes time, says Sydorick, "because in California there's the geologist, there's the engineer, there's the city, there's all these people. I knew it was going to be a huge

The interior of Sydorick's favorite Alfa contrasts with the color of the stone wall at the back of the new addition. Sydorick's car buddies comment that his decorating taste is on a higher level than most. **Phil Berg**

project." Seventy-five truckloads of earth were excavated, and 50 were dumped in the grass courtyard to use as backfill once the massive concrete footings and walls were poured.

If there's an award for the most effort to gain space, David Sydorick and his wife, Ginny, who is equally as passionate about classic Italian cars, win it. The expan-

sion burrowed into the mountain only behind the original three-car space under the guesthouse and not behind the single-car addition Sydorick added in 1994.

"It was the only space I could have. I'd have had a 25-foot retaining wall if we tried to expand behind the addition. This was the most amount of garage for the least amount of money that I could do, and without creating a huge mess. And I couldn't push back anymore into the mountain because I'd hit the property lines—the wall would just get higher and higher and higher."

The new back wall of the garage and a shelf across the mirrored side wall are covered with large pieces of stone, artfully placed. "I picked out all the stone, and I placed all the stone," says Sydorick. "The supplier delivers pallets, and on the top are the big ones, and underneath are little pieces of nothing. So I had to get a lot of pallets and pick out the big ones. I didn't want the big ones down below because the cars would be there. I want the big ones here so you could see them. Same thing on the shelf."

Surprisingly, the stone took only two days to install, thanks to a crew of four. The masons, too, were familiar with the place because they were the same crew that had sided the house 10 years earlier and then matched the workshop addition a few years later.

The floors of the addition match the outside court-yard and the floors of the existing garages, which feature a relatively simple stamped-concrete treatment, molded to resemble huge slabs of stone. The stamped-concrete floor is stained with green between the large squares, to match the grass in the courtyard. Every detail in the garage has been designed to Sydorick's tastes.

"I wanted the trophy case over here behind this wall so you won't see it when you look in," he explains. "It will be very clean." He wondered about installing skylights above the new addition but decided against it because the addition has a flat roof, and "flat skylights always seem to be dirty."

"It feels great to be in here," Sydorick says, a week after all the major work is finished. The floor at the back

This smaller garage, attached to the side of the house, can hold three more cars while Sydorick's daily drivers are parked on the circular drive to the front door of his house. **Phil Berg**

After the addition, those four special cars line up against the back stone wall, with room for several more.
Phil Berg

wall of the newly expanded garage is eight inches higher than at the doors. It's not for drainage but for a gravity assist, so one person can roll a car into the courtyard before starting it. "If you start them inside," explains Sydorick, "they leak oil."

Car people, Sydorick says, are born with the gene. "You start working with cars before you have cars if you really have the gene." Sydorick says he began pursuing his car passion in his early teens. He built a tube-frame go kart with a Harley engine and gearbox in it. It had bucket seats and full brakes and a suspended front axle. "I'm not sure I ever drove it, but I created it and built it."

"My first car was a 1958 Chevy Impala convertible, and I ended up putting a 409 in it," he explains. "And I had a 1957 T-bird with a 406 in it. They were street cars at the time. Then I went to college, and we had sports cars. I gained an enlarged appreciation of cars in college."

Sydorick didn't start collecting the Italian specials until 1990, when he restored a Ferrari. In 1994, he drove his first Mille Miglia, the 1,000-mile granddaddy of vintage races, from Brescia to Rome. "The Italians have an unbelievable passion for the automobile," he concluded after the event.

After that he developed his passion for Zagato in particular. Of 19 Maseratis built by Zagato, only one had a bubble roof, the trademark Zagato had built into his Alfas. The serial number of the lone bubble Maserati was 21, and Sydorick found that the owner had the car in southern California, at a restoration shop.

The owner was planning to move back to Sicily and ship the car back there but delayed his own return. After a few years, Sydorick convinced the owner to sell him the car. So he flew to Sicily to look at it, and finally he found it buried under construction materials in a small dirt-floor garage that had a three-foot brick wall built in front of it for security. After the owner's relatives broke down the wall, Sydorick brought the car back to California and spent two and a half years restoring it.

Now Sydorick actively drives it in long-distance tours around the world that are run by classic collectors. He's driven his cars in China (a 1932 Alfa 1750) and South America (an Alfa Giulietta), as well as the Italian and California versions of the Mille Miglia.

"I've never raced—never thought about it," he says, although he has several unique hot rods besides his Italian cars—an integration he considers completely natural. To Sydorick, the Boyd Coddington Aluma

A Fiat and a custom hot rod peek out from their covers in the workshop addition, which is adjacent to the main garage. **Phil Berg**

Coupe hot rod is equally as artful as a Zagato-designed Alfa Romeo.

Even though Sydorick believes you can't have too many cars, he's tried living with his cars off-site. "You can store them many places, but then you end up not using them. You need staff. There is no staff here. I had rental space away from here, and it just didn't work, and everyone told me it wouldn't work.

"The hardest part of the expansion was living with the dirt. It's all gone now. I spend a lot of time in here—it's lovely. It came out the way I expected. I have about 15 cars. This is how many cars I can have." Now he's done.

9

Al
Wiseman

Classic
Car Castle

This collector got it
right: First garage,
then house

"I tried that retirement bit for about six months and actually went nuts. So I decided to turn a hobby into a business," says Al Wiseman, a car collector whose 120 cars are shoehorned into several custom garage buildings in Florida.

As president of Airborne Express until 1991, Wiseman used to buy all the airplanes for that company. Now he'd like to buy a Tucker, the rear-engine classic car made famous by a flamboyant inventor and by Hollywood.

"Ever since I was a kid, I loved cars. My father was a mechanic, my stepfather was a mechanic. I was raised in

Previous page: Often the garage holds so many cars that Al Wiseman doesn't have an exact count, but it always looks like Santa's workshop. Michael Stewart

that environment, and I never had the money to have anything nice. Time went on, I had the money to get into it, and I did. Lost my head at one point and got carried away. The more money I made, the more I got carried away."

He got carried away when he was living in Ohio, near the headquarters for the aviation division of Airborne

Every dream garage needs an antique gas pump. **Michael Stewart**

"I'm one of those guys that's got his priorities straight," says Al Wiseman, who built this garage before building his house on the property. Michael Stewart

Express. "The first car I owned was a 1950 Studebaker Skylark coupe," he recalls. Later, he bought a 1959 Corvette and raced it in road races throughout the 1970s, mostly at tracks in Ohio. At the same time, he was climbing the corporate ranks as an aircraft engineer. His time for racing diminished, and he gradually began collecting cars. "I bought a 1928 Buick in the 1970s, but I didn't get really serious about collecting until the 1980s."

When Wiseman retired from Airborne Express, he started other businesses, one of them an aviation company

in Ohio, that he later moved to Florida. By then, he had a collection of 25 cars. "I left most of them up in Ohio because I didn't have room down in Florida to put them."

The long-distance relationship has its disadvantages. "When they're that far away and you can't attend to them constantly, they deteriorate a little bit." At that point, Wiseman realized he needed some large buildings so that he could move his collection to Florida.

Wiseman's first garage was completed in 1996, but he realized it wasn't big enough for his collection, so he

Many of Wiseman's cars are domestics and range from these muscle cars to older classics from the 1920s to the 1940s. **Michael Stewart**

built second and third garages behind the first one. "There are two buildings. One has four or five doors, and one has five doors—I forget.

"I'm one of those guys that got his priorities straight. I built my garage first and built the house next door second. Actually, my wife calls my house the life-support system for my shop."

His "shop" now is made up of three buildings, which contain about 120 cars and 55 motorcycles and scooters. This doesn't include the hundred or so cars for sale at the

Capital Car Store, one of the businesses he started. It sells mostly American classics, 1972 and earlier.

The Capital Car Store, which is a few miles from his home, was built in 1997, after he began building his personal garages. A year later he built the Classic Car Restoration Center, which is separate from Capital Car and one of the largest restoration businesses in the country. Wiseman started it with the Brand brothers, who had become known in the area for high-quality Corvette restorations.

Wiseman found these antique air pressure gauges at swap meets. **Michael Stewart**

Inside Wiseman's collection of garages is his collection of cars. "It's a huge variation, my collection, and hard to describe. I have all the way from an 1893 Duryea to 1950s and 1960s cars. I also like the big iron from the mid-1920s to the mid-1940s—Packards, Duesenbergs, Auburns, Cords, that type of car," he says.

Most of Wiseman's cars are American made—or partly American. "I have a Rolls I'm converting over to a Chevy engine." He found a 1971 Silver Shadow that had been converted to Chevy V-8 power once, but the workmanship was bad and the car was unreliable, so he revamped it. "I tried to integrate the positive ground [wiring] with negative-ground wiring, but it just didn't work." He rewired the car and added new power windows, a digital instrument panel, and a new GM steering column. "Everything is changed except the body shell," he says. "I do all my own work. I was raised as a mechanic, in that environment."

Another project Wiseman is working on is a 1963 Corvette split-window coupe he's completely restoring for shows. "I had that car many, many years, and I used to race it. I'm taking it back to factory specs." He's also got a 1957 Chevy Cameo pickup truck he's converting to a new Cadillac Northstar drivetrain.

A car that gets a lot of visitors' attention is the Batmobile from the movie *Batman Forever*. Wiseman says it's not legal to drive on the street and that the movie production company won't allow him to use it to promote his business without its permission. "They still control the image of that car," he says.

Wiseman says he can't sell any photos of the Batmobile car, since the purchase price from Warner Brothers did not include image rights. **Michael Stewart**

Wiseman takes pride in his 1933 Packard, with 11,000 original miles: "It's magnificent. I like the unusual. If you see my collection, you see a lot of one-of-a kind stuff. You see a lot of rare stuff in there . . . . The unusual is what I go after, usually." He restored a 1931 Cadillac and a 1930 Cord boattail speedster that's one of only three in existence. Some of his cars are preserved and are not driven on the street.

After more than 20 years of being a serious collector, Wiseman now is focused on one elusive machine: "I've been trying to find a Tucker, and I just haven't found one worth jumping on at the right price. I thought I was going to get one a few weeks ago, but the reserve was just too high. You're talking $200,000 for a Tucker." A year ago,

Wiseman was able to find the Stanley Steamer he wanted, which had been almost as elusive as the Tucker.

Wiseman designed his garages himself. "I'd seen some other shops up in Ohio, and you kind of learn what you need—the equipment you need, the space you need, and how you want to proceed. By the time I came down to Florida and built this, I had the money to do it like I wanted." He allocated space to install a complete machine shop, with cutting machines, including a plasma metal cutter. He also has welders, sheet metal tools, and complete fabrication facilities. "You name it, it's pretty well here. I'm one of those guys who hates to stop in the middle of a job because I don't have a tool or I don't have a machine, or I don't have the equipment to do a particular job."

Even though he has a large restoration shop with the same facilities at the Classic Car Restoration Center, he has his own paint shop in his garage. "When I do something, I don't want to do it with anyone else, whether it's paint or bodywork—you name it."

The floors of Wiseman's garages are a spectacular checkerboard pattern made of porcelain floating on a layer of Teflon and a layer of cork on top of a concrete pad. This was done so the floor won't crack, even if the concrete below does. He's found the porcelain to be impervious to stains and marks, and it's easy to clean.

Wiseman is practical about keeping his hobby of restoring his personal collection separate from the restoration business. "I don't restore cars for the car store. You can't make money restoring a car today. The 40-car work backlog we have at the car store is all customers with a particular car they want restored. I tell them, 'Look, I'll sell you one already done a whole lot cheaper than a restoration will cost you,' but they say 'No, I want this car.' Maybe they owned it when they were younger or something."

Wiseman's favorite street cars are a 1956 Chevy convertible, a 1957 Chevy, a 1964 Cadillac convertible,

Wiseman holds twice-a-month tours of the garage for car clubs that gather from around the country.
Michael Stewart

and a 1932 Duesenberg. "I take the '33 Packard out to dinner occasionally, but the Cord is strictly a trailer queen," he adds. "I've got a '53 Caddy Coupe de Ville I used to drive, but it's got 20,000 miles on it, and it's all original—including the tires, which are dry-rotted."

Several times each month, car clubs call Wiseman and request tours of his garage, which he gives often. "The collection is so diverse. I've got a little of everything: old-fashioned, steam-powered popcorn machines and peanut roasters, old player pianos and dime-store rides, and people hear about it and want to see it."

One of the garages has a covered patio in the corner. "The shops are pretty full, so I stick the cars I drive fairly often out there. I'm out of room already, but I'm not going to build any buildings for a while. So that's my problem. I sold off my Camaro pace car collection several years ago to make room for my other cars."

Still, Wiseman plans to go to auctions and swap meets to find more cars. "I'm going this weekend to a bid auction. It's got a lot of neat old cars, and I might get a couple. I don't know if I've got a loose nut, or what it is. It's a passion."

Part 2

Real-
World
Garages

10

Ken Gross

A New Start

Building a garage
from scratch can lead
to bigger things

"It's wonderful to have a workable space," says Ken Gross, a hot rod expert who is as astute about the dull parts of the auto industry as he is about the genuine art of the automobile.

Gross took time out from being an auto industry journalist to become the curator of the Petersen Museum in Los Angeles, the car nut's Smithsonian. He was tasked with overseeing the care and welfare of irreplaceable wheeled works of American history for four years, before recently returning to the world of magazine writing and to the East Coast, where he grew up in the 1960s.

Section opener: Tom Sparks, who has spent more than 50 years tinkering, collecting, and racing cars, has filled his garage with auto memorabilia. Phil Berg

Previous page: The home for Ken Gross' three classic autos sits peacefully on a hill overlooking a pond in Virginia. A full apartment above the garage was built without closets so that the assessor would not count it as living space. **Michael Stewart**

The Ford roadster on the lift is another of Gross' favorites and is powered by a Ford flathead V-8. **Michael Stewart**

An early passion for 1950s Ford hot rods steered Gross to collect a wall full of intake manifolds that are used only for decoration. Michael Stewart

His collection of almost 100 intake manifolds for Ford flathead V-8 engines finally has a dignified home too, now that Gross built a new colonial house with a gracious three-car garage on five acres of rolling hills in Virginia.

"The first thing I did was pegboard the whole back wall, and I probably will put up another wall of it because the manifolds seem to be breeding. Partly it adds to the ambiance, and it's a nice, safe place. We don't have earthquakes here, so the likelihood of something falling down is low," he explains. Above the garage is a large room that's finished like a one-room apartment, although local zoning codes say it can't be used as a bedroom because it has no closets. As his home was being built, Gross had planned to use this space to store his massive car-magazine collection, but when he moved in, he found the second floor of the garage to be too small and turned his basement into a library instead.

The Woody is original, and the Ford roadster on the lift is just as clean underneath as on top. Yet Gross has driven the car on the road hundreds of miles to shows. Michael Stewart

"Having a nice garage, which isn't fabulous but better than some, means that you can conveniently work on a car if you want to work on it, clean it, detail it, paint it—you can do all that stuff," says Gross. "I like that it's a great place to put my intake manifolds and all my other automotive art."

Now Gross hosts gatherings of fellow flathead V-8 lovers in his new garage, something he was never able to do before. "I'm really a nut for flatheads. I'm writing a flathead book. I was always fascinated with the engine, and I don't know if it was because I was speed equipment–deprived as a child or what. I used to

look through issues of *Hot Rod*, and I just wanted all of it. And now I've got a lot of it."

Until he built his new house, Gross says he never really had a great space to work in. "Our home in California wasn't big enough. I usually could keep one car at home, in a pinch two, but basically I used to keep one car at the museum at times." That's clearly not enough room for a guy who has owned a Ferrari 275 GTB and a Dino, five Morgans, a Jaguar XK150, a Lamborghini, and a corral of motorcycles, including several Vincents and three Ducatis.

When he found the site in Virginia, the foundation for the garage had already been poured, but Gross was able to specify the height of the roof so that he could install a lift. He also was able to plumb the garage for a gas heater and upgrade the electrical system for extra circuits and a 220-volt outlet for a welder and the lift. "You can run a lift on 110 volts, but they just work a lot better and a lot faster on 220."

When he moved in, he painted the floor with epoxy, a standard practice with garage aficionados. "My garage is pretty small by comparison to some, but it's got everything I need. It's a happy space," he says. "I mean, I go out there and I see all this stuff on the walls that I've been able to accumulate."

He keeps a heater set at 55 degrees in the winter. "When I want to spend a couple hours, it isn't going out in the garage and freezing to death. It's like enjoying the way you would work on a car in California. I highly recommend heat. If I had to do it all over, I would run water piping under the floors and have radiant heat. But it doesn't get quite as cold here as it does in other places."

The next step to finishing the garage is to install cabinets. "I have a compressor so I can run my tools, but cabinetry would be cool," he says. Not just any cabinets, but special garage cabinets he's seen at trade shows and the Specialty Equipment Market Association (SEMA) show. "I like everything in *Griot's* catalog," he says. "They have stuff you didn't think you needed until you saw their catalog. You say, 'I gotta have that.' I used their kit for two-step epoxy floor coverings."

Gross inventories the equipment in his garage: "I have power tools, impact wrenches, the lift, a decent jack, the facility to change oil, one of those extendable drain machines. While I don't have welding equipment, and it's been a long time since I've done any welding, I want whatever it is I need there, and I want to have room to work." He saw a sandblasting cabinet at the annual Hershey classic car show in Pennsylvania that he wants.

"I'm trying to convince my wife, Trish, that a blast cabinet is the perfect thing to buy me for Christmas."

The new garage is also giving Gross thoughts of doing a restoration project. The prospect is slowly forming in his mind. "Years ago, I used to have a three-wheel Morgan, and I did quite a bit of work on it, overhauled the engine. Growing up in high school, I did a lot of work on my cars. Over the years, I've tried to do as much as I can do. I'd love to do a fairly extensive restoration that my eight-year-old son Jake could watch and have it be a little part of his own small world. I think it would be a fun thing to work on together. If I did that, I could put one of my cars somewhere else and have the room to do the restoration."

As he thinks about it, his restoration idea gets more specific. "When you're taking a car apart, you run the risk, if you're keeping stuff in different places, of things getting lost and confused and mixed," he says. "To me, the ideal is a place to put a chassis and close alongside it tables and racks to put up all the stuff, and carefully label it because it may be a year or two before you put it back together again."

The idea of a project has led Gross to the thought of buying another car, one that would need some work. "I haven't bought a new car since we moved in here. I'm looking for a 1940 Ford coupe, and there will be room for it with the setup I have. As Jake gets older, I'm hoping this '40 Ford will be a car that needs a great deal of work over a period of time."

The house sits on a steep slope overlooking a large pond in front, and in back is a courtyard that gradually rises up a hill. Already Gross is thinking of expanding the garage. "We have five acres, so my hope is to extend this garage backward, which would work on my property and would actually look kind of nice," he says.

He hasn't ruled out building another structure either, but right now the current floor plan is working. "For my little collection of old Fords and manifolds—and I have an understanding wife who doesn't mind parking outside—this is a great place."

11

Bill Hammerstein

The Fun Run Place

A former pool house, this garage offers picturesque parking

If Bill Hammerstein could bottle his car enthusiasm and give it away, we'd all be instant addicts. Children with candy are no happier than "Hammer," as his friends call him, when he's behind the wheel of a classic sports car. A land developer in California, he and wife, Marcie, just sent their youngest away to college, and "I'm not ready to retire," he says. "I'd like to spend more time doing car things. We'd like to go to Monaco and see the race, go to Le Mans and see that. My wife is a bigger car person than I am. Now with our daughter gone, we can do more of those things."

Hammerstein bought his current house and garage in 1989, but it looked nothing like the structure today. "At that time, it had this funny little garage that was half garage and half little pool house, and you entered it from the street, not the alley."

After a year, Hammerstein remodeled the little single-car garage so that the door opened onto the alley. Then he closed off the driveway leading from the street and turned it into a garden. Between the little garage and the pool was a small pool house. "This old rickety place," he recalls. He completely remodeled the pool house and added a bathroom and a bar. Then he filled the garage and the pool house with car memorabilia and photos of Hammerstein and his wife and daughter on sports car drives with folks like Carroll Shelby, Dan Gurney, and other famous car guys.

Previous page: The glow of a southern California sky outlines Bill Hammerstein's backyard garage. Inside, three of his cars are framed by French doors left over from when the structure was a pool house. **Phil Berg**

Even when the garage only had space for one car, it was still a hangout for Hammerstein and his enthusiast friends. **Dennis Adler**

"I enclosed the pool house a few years ago and put in those windows and the glass doors because I thought my daughter was going to use it . . . but she didn't," Hammerstein says. "After a couple of years, I finally said, 'To heck with it, I'm going to tear the pool house out and I'm going to make it into a two-car garage.' "

The new two-car structure kept the French doors and windows from the pool house, but Hammerstein lowered the floor so that a lift would fit on one side. Completed in 2001, the garage has a double door that opens into the alley and a floor tiled in a black-and-white checkerboard pattern. The vaulted ceiling contains large, threaded steel tie bars so that the structure will survive an earthquake. Hammerstein would love to expand the garage even more, but the building is restricted on one side by the zoning setback and on the other side by the pool.

"Now I put three cars in there and four or five over at my other storage area. I keep at home what I think are the show cars—the Cobra, the Daytona, the SL. I drive them all. Last Sunday we went up the coast for a drive in the SL."

The cars Hammerstein stores include a 1962 327 Corvette he's owned for more than 20 years. "That's the car I wanted when I graduated from college, but my parents gave me GM stock instead. So I bought it 20 years ago. I have a '64 Porsche SC Cabriolet. Then we have a '39 Ford street rod with a 350 Chevy engine in it. Then I have a Typhoon that was my daughter's car here. It's bright yellow, and I'm going to restore it. When she went to college, we got her a 3-series BMW to use. She's the third one to go to Colorado University, and she's having a ball." he says. The license plate on his Corvette reads "CU 62" because the school also is his alma mater. "About every two years, I have all the cars detailed."

Hammerstein has toyed with plans to put another two-car garage next to the existing one, but that would mean taking out the pool and replacing it with a small lap pool. To avoid that, Hammerstein has considered, very briefly, other options. "My wife told me we should buy the house next door and turn the whole house into a garage. Gut the whole thing and have one house and a garage next door."

He passed on the plans to expand his garage space at home. "I would love to put all of my cars in a garage at home. But I figured if I ever wanted to sell the house, a second garage would be too much garage space for the person who would want to buy the house." Additionally, his other cars are stored just five minutes away, which is also five minutes from his office. "Living and working five minutes apart makes life very simple. I don't have to look at a commute. You tend to work longer and smarter."

The photo wall carried over from the old garage to the new one has pictures of him and his cars on drives and tracks and at shows. It gives the impression that everyone Hammerstein knows is a car nut, including his wife and daughter, and that it's his entire life away from the office. That's mostly true.

"Every Sunday I get up before my family gets up and I head out at 7:30 and go for a drive. I was talking to some other guys and they said they do the same thing, so I figured I'd organize it." Hammerstein formed a group that meets every third Sunday morning to take "fun runs." "There's about 20 guys on the e-mail list, and we usually get anywhere from 10 to 15 guys on those Sundays." The group drives up the Pacific coast and takes different back roads through the mountains and hills, driving everything from hot rods to concours-winning Ferraris.

"Some guys said we should stop for breakfast, but we say this is a driving thing—if you want to go to breakfast, go before or after, but we're on the road at 8:30. We're usually back home by noon."

In addition to the fun runs, Hammerstein is an active member of a group called the Checkered Flag 200, which was originally formed to organize car events and

Leaving the French doors from the pool house intact, workers dug out the floor and poured a slab to create a two-space garage without disturbing the checkered tile from the original single space. **Bill Hammerstein**

fundraisers for the Petersen Museum. The name refers to how many people the group initially thought would join them, but membership is now about 350, says Hammerstein. Every month these guys drive somewhere, too. "When you live in this weather, you can take your car out every weekend," he says.

This list of drives Hammerstein has planned rivals the NASCAR schedule. He's does two organized drives each month, and then he does four large, 1,000-mile drives every year. "The June California Classic we do, then the Concours on Rodeo. Then we do the Copper State rally in Arizona. We're planning a Corvette thing at

In the new garage, a photo wall becomes a gathering spot whenever Hammerstein has a party. The roof beams are tied together with steel rods. So far, the garage has survived one large earthquake unscathed. **Phil Berg**

the Petersen, too. We'll have about 500 Corvettes, one from each year, and some special GS models. Then I'm hoping I get accepted to the Colorado Grand this year. If I don't get the Colorado Grand, we'll do the Texas 1000. It's a fun group of guys. I just like to drive my cars. I'm driving all the time."

Hammerstein is shortly going to wrap up his six-year tenure as a member of the Beverly Hills Traffic and Parking Commission. "We've done a lot in the last six years," he says. "Beverly Hills is a small city, about 10,000 people, but every day 150,000 people drive through here." Because the streets are crowded, commuters used to cut down alleys and snake through side streets. Hammerstein proposed a right-turn rule and also helped get the city's traffic lights synchronized with those of surrounding Los Angeles "so you can drive through Beverly Hills and not have to stop."

"We have a huge valet problem here because all the restaurants have valets, and you're always dealing with valet problems. You have some Mister Big in his Rolls Royce, and he hands the parker $20 and says, 'I want to park out front,' but you can't do that because everyone can't park out front." Hammerstein has planning expertise from his land development business, and he's also on the board of directors for local the St. John's Hospital. "I like to get involved with that and give a little back."

Originally from Kansas, Hammerstein has lived in California for more than 40 years. "When we consider moving, we always reconsider. Where would we go where we could find car guys like this so close?"

12

Chuck Higgins

A Workaholic's Vision

Two years
and 30,000
nails pay off

"There was a period of about 15 years where I wasn't doing anything but work," says Chuck Higgins, who moved to central Florida 22 years ago for college and stayed to start a software business. "I'm a man of very modest means. I spend every available dollar on my cars."

After those 15 years of self-described workaholism in the software engineering industry, Higgins was ready to explode, and the outlet he chose was building his dream garage—a four-place structure that follows the lines of his house.

Higgins bought the house with a two-car conventional garage attached, as well as a carport added to that. Like a true car nut, he felt three covered spaces was not enough. The three-acre lot is in a wooded subdivision, and before he built the new garage, he had to clear enough trees so the new garage would fit next to the house. "If you want to do the math, I have more garage space than house space," he beams. "Between the existing two-car garage and the carport and the new shop, it's more than 3,000 square feet."

The shape of the garage is based on Higgins' house, a modern single-story with tall ridge lines and vertical sky windows. "I wanted to copy the sky windows," he explains. Height is important to Higgins, for a feeling of space and to be able to handle big car projects in the future. Economics was another factor: "If I ever go to sell the house, somebody else might not have the same desire to have that much garage space," he adds. "So they can convert it to a mother-in-law living space. You can easily take those big garage doors out and convert it, and it won't look like a square box."

A second design element borrowed from the house is the large bay window that surrounds the workbench at the back of the garage. "I've got that same detail in my breakfast nook," he says.

Finished in 1998, the building took a year and a half to complete. "The only thing I contracted out was a

slab," says Higgins. "I started off building it entirely myself, and then with my friends' help. People you work with are great for help, especially if you're the boss."

Higgins designed the garage, a four-place building with half of it double-height so that he could put in a lift. "I drew the entire plans up myself, took them down, and got them approved, so I actually got permits and stuff," he adds.

Higgins had drawn his plans to include a small attic that he could access from a pulldown staircase. "It frees up floor space, and you can still easily climb up to the attic," he explains.

However, when he presented his plans to the company that was supplying the roof trusses for the garage, it suggested raising the roof of the lower section garage about one foot. This would enable him to convert the attic space into a loft. "The low half was just going to be a regular garage," he recalls. "But since we kicked up the trusses, we got more free attic space. They designed it with no center post, so you end up with a really neat space up there."

The garage's quality construction is a source of satisfaction for Higgins. "I used 30,000 nails," he recalls. "There's either 5,000 or 6,000 nails in a case, and we threw all the empty nail cartons in a corner as we were building the place. Compressed-air nail guns make it so easy to put in a lot of nails. One squeeze of the trigger and that's it."

Being handy with tools, Higgins wired the new garage for his 240-volt TIG welder and air compressor. He put outlets in the walls and over the workbench every two feet, nearly triple what the electrical code calls for. "It's still not enough outlets," he adds. Another work-

The garage holds most of Higgins' cars. His rock-climbing Jeep stays under a separate carport.
Michael Stewart

bench in the low section of the garage is built around his radial arm saw and drill press. He closes those tools off with curtains to keep the garage looking cleaner.

Changing from workaholic to car hobbyist happened at the same time Higgins built his new garage. Ten years earlier, he bought a Porsche 911, but in the past couple of years he's turned it into a competition car. He's also added a Viper, Mercedes sedan, and Jeep CJ5 outfitted for Rubicon duty to his fleet. "I've

got a Swiss army knife collection," he explains. "There's a car for every purpose. I'm in a Jeep club, and I take it out West and to the beaches. It's got a roll cage that's been tested in a mud gulch in northern Florida."

He also joined the Porsche club two years ago. "The 911 is my track car. I drive it on the street often because it's still street legal." Even with 200,000 miles on the odometer, the car has no door dings and the paint is original. "I've been able to keep it in pristine condition,"

The company that supplied Higgins' roof trusses suggested raising the roof 12 inches higher than the original design to create a storage loft at the top of the garage. Michael Stewart

he says with pride, "but I punish it regularly. I've been really lucky about avoiding contact. I've got rock chips, but rock chips are OK because they're badges of honor."

The Porsche was likely the root of Higgins' current car hobby, which began when his father gave him a Karmann Ghia when he was in high school in New York.

"I was really lucky, but I just used it to get back and forth to work so I could start buying more cars," he explains, "I would buy cars with a little bit of body damage and fix them and sell them and move up.

"When I got the Porsche, I had to make a financial decision. The only way I could afford that car was if I did

The bay window workbench is a design element from the breakfast nook in the house. **Michael Stewart**

all the work. If you buy a six-year-old 911 and if anything goes wrong and you take it to your mechanic, you might as well buy a new one. You'll go broke really fast. I bit the bullet and bought the factory manuals—they cost me something like twelve hundred bucks. That was it. I said, 'If anything breaks, I'm fixing it.' "

With the new garage, Higgins has seven spaces and only four cars, a ratio that's rare in the car nut world. He expects to fill up the spaces. His local Porsche club uses his garage for technical classes every month. He also has a friend using the shop to convert an automatic Mustang to a manual.

What he's learned is that building his own garage wasn't as expensive as he thought. "Based on loose records, it cost only about $25,000," he says. "If you shop around for materials and stuff, and do the labor yourself, it's not that expensive. You're talking about putting a roof on for $1,500 in materials, but it's a lot of labor. And it's tough putting the shingles on in all that heat.

"It does take a lot more time than you think. You don't have a crew of eight people, so you do have to budget a lot more time than you think. Drywall is extremely time-consuming." He compares it to fixing the bent cars he has acquired: "Drywall is a simplified form of bodywork, but look at the square footage that you have to cover. Either you finish it rough and you

The floor area is slightly larger than a standard four-car garage, providing space for motorcycles.
Michael Stewart

Welding is among the bodywork skills Higgins uses for repairs. **Michael Stewart**

have to cover all the walls with compound, or you finish it smooth." He chose the latter, but the result is exactly what he wanted. "I've kind of kept it trinket-free. I'm kind of happy I don't have a vintage gas pump.

"Everybody that comes over to my house says, 'I want this.' I tell them to build their own garage. It's not that hard when I look back on it. But I can see why more people don't do this because it is a big commitment.

"You can say that because I have the shop it's given

me more opportunity to work on the cars," he says. "I kind of took a break from cars when I was in a furious career-building mode up until about 1998, at which point I could slow down a little bit. That gave me time to get the cars and enjoy this stuff.

"There's nothing better than waking up on Saturday morning and not have to go anywhere and do anything, and then hang out in the garage. Don't you wish every morning was like Saturday morning?"

13

Peter McCoy

A Classy Workshop

With the kids away, this collector finally has a space to play

If details determine the quality of a builder, then Peter McCoy's six-car garage reflects its owner's ability as a professional builder. There are lots of lights and windows, cabinets of furniture quality, and a hard-wood-covered pit for maintenance, all facing a pleasing courtyard for this six-car garage tucked up high in the California hills.

"I'm in the construction business, so for me it's maybe a little easier than what some of the other guys want to do," McCoy explains. "I wouldn't normally install this kind of wood, but I was tearing down a house and it was old paneling in that house, and I just used it here."

McCoy is a member of the collector group that doesn't want their cars farther than 200 feet from their home. "It is of no interest to me to have a car stored off-site. My involvement is more instantaneous. I want to get up in the morning and say, 'I want to take the blue Porsche.' Driving these cars is a spontaneous thing," he adds, "and if you store them off-site, you say, 'I've got to get in the car and I have to go down there and get a

Once McCoy's children left home, he expanded his garage to hold his sports car collection. **Phil Berg**

A tidy workbench is just big enough for the repairs and maintenance McCoy does on his cars. **Phil Berg**

car.' Then you have to remember to get your sunglasses and anything else you need when you're driving, and you have to ask, 'Did I remember to bring my hat?' "

McCoy's six-car garage is actually two garages: the first a four-car garage built in 1989 and the second a two-car addition constructed in 2000. "We've lived in that house for 40-some years. At one time, there was a small garage that was more accommodated to storing unused household products than it was to storing cars.

But I didn't like leaving cars out, so when the opportunity presented itself for me to redesign parts of the house, I decided I would have a lot of storage space and a lot of garage space.

"Had I known when I built the garage where I was going with the cars I wanted to get, I may have done some things differently. I may have made it deeper. I may have put a different roll top garage door on it. I would have framed the roofing differently to make it easier to put a lift system in. I can do some of that now—it's just more of a pain that I didn't plan ahead for an eventuality that may or may not come."

The hallway between the four-car section and the two-car addition contains a photo wall of family pictures along with a bathroom and closets.

"I never liked lifts because of the appearance, but lately I've seen some that really look nice. When you go into a garage, you don't like to see a bunch of lifts. But I may wind up there one day," McCoy says, because he sees himself potentially short on space. "As I got the other cars that I liked, that's when I added the other little two-car garage."

Originally, McCoy's home in the hills had a small, detached garage at the side. He decided to build the first new garage from the ground up. "We had an architect for it. The evolution of the garage was that the kids were at home, and they were both driving cars in high school, and I just didn't like cars in the driveway. So we designed the four-car garage really as a family garage. Then the kids grew up, took their cars away, and we found something to fill the void."

*A bathroom and storage space connect the two buildings that make up McCoy's garage. **Phil Berg***

The wood paneling in this section was rescued from a house being torn down. The plank-covered pit on the left facilitates work under the cars. Phil Berg

The "something" was a collection of classic sports cars, and it soon grew larger than the space. "I have five cars now, older sports cars, then some family cars," he says. "I get what I like and I keep it and take care of it. I'm a custodian. There's a 1965 Morgan Plus 4, a great fun car to drive. There's the 1957 Speedster, there's a 1954 XK120, there's a 275 GTS Ferrari. It's a 1965. And a 300SL Roadster, which is a 1958." A year after the two bays were added to the garage, McCoy bought the Porsche, but the other cars started to gather when the kids began moving out.

You could call McCoy's car enthusiasm typical, especially now that he's an empty-nester. "I've always kind of been interested in cars as a hobby. For a lot of us who grew up in the 1950s, there was just something fun

about them. Today you have video games, but the 1950s were all cars. We would try to make them go faster, experiment with them. The first car I had was a 1930 Model A coupe. It was a real simple car to work on. You break a transmission, and there used to be a little junkyard in West Hollywood, and you just went up there to get another one. You'd trade it in for 10 or 20 bucks."

Another early impression came from wartime Detroit iron. "After the Model A, I had a 1941 Buick convertible, just beat to hell. It had no top. I thought the car was neat because it was the first car I had with two carburetors. It had no suspension, but it was relatively quick."

"My first civilized car was a 1950 Ford convertible." McCoy recalls that this was the point at which he took a hiatus from the car hobby. He started a family and

grew his business. "I did have a wonderful 1968 Morgan, and that was when I was first married. We had to sell it because the kids came along. The Morgan was my first import sports car. It was just a super car."

Even though McCoy has now acquired a bevy of clean European classic sports cars, he has no prejudices against domestics. In fact, while his family was still growing, he jumped back into the car hobby with a 1928

Model A roadster that was a basket case. "I bought that car in 1974 and did a ground-up restoration. The kids liked it because it had a rumble seat. I kept it for 10 years."

His current collection didn't begin until the late 1980s, just before he built the four-car garage. The first car he bought was the Jaguar XK120. "They all have a unique driving experience. The Jaguar is so different than the Porsche," he says. "The Jaguar has such an

and on all those challenging roads, we'll take the Porsche."

Part of McCoy misses the hot rod experience, and he's thinking he might get another one, after 20 years without one. "There's a threshold for the number of cars you can have until it turns into a full-time job," he says. "No, I'm not at that threshold, and I'm not sure I want to get there. I love to drive them, and if it's something I can work on, fine, and if it isn't, then it's gone. I have some guys who help take care of the cars. I send my Ferrari to Wisconsin for work. I'm not a big fan of the newer Ferraris. I like the 1950s and 1960s. There's always something to be doing on the cars."

McCoy's a hands-on collector, however, and does his own maintenance on his five special cars in the garage. "I never pictured it as a collection," he says. "You know, we've all been in these unbelievable garages, and I just never pictured mine that way. All the stuff I have, I like to drive and have fun in out on the road."

McCoy spends time in his garage by himself or with other car guys he goes with on driving tours, but he says parties at his house don't usually wind up in the garage. "We have a big family kitchen, and if we really have a big party, then the catering people have to set up in the garage," he explains. "Some garages are more conducive to wandering around during a party. I'm a little self-conscious [about] having people out there when they come to party, unless it's the car guys."

McCoy says he's not so worried about guests spilling drinks on his cars as about not wanting to look like a showoff. "My stuff is pretty ordinary stuff. There's nothing in there that's unique or rare." Hundreds of Jaguar fans and other car nuts would heartily disagree.

incredible sound and rhythm when it's cruising—at least to my ear. It's a great driving experience."

McCoy speaks about planning a driving trip as if he's looking through a closet, picking an outfit. "If you're going on a mountain rally, the Jaguar's probably not the car to take. But if you're just going up to Otis Chandler's museum or something like that, and you're just going up highways, it's a great driving experience. In the mountains

14

Lynn Park

A Place for a Fanatic

Whether for Cobras
or pinball machines,
collections need space

ynn Park is likely the most passionate Cobra fan in the country. Cobra creator and legendary racer Carroll Shelby often calls the 59-year-old Park to chat about the cars, which Shelby built from 1962 to 1965 and are considered the archetypal American sports car.

Park is so committed to the care and storage of his current collection of nine Cobras that he removed the swimming pool from his backyard to make room for a larger garage. He'd have more Cobras and a bigger garage, except for one thing. "My wife's got all her roses planted behind the garage, so another building isn't going to happen."

Previous page: Neighbors have used Lynn Park's garage as a backdrop for Christmas card photos, although the place more regularly sees club gatherings. Phil Berg

Cobra fan Park still dreams. "If I saw a lot near here that would enable me to build a smaller house with a bigger garage, that would be ideal. I would love to buy more Cobras. No one has a big enough garage. My dream is 3,000 square feet of house and 3,000 square feet of garage."

Though the antique dragster isn't legal in any racing classes, Park makes room for it in his garage, which also holds nine Cobras and a Willys. Phil Berg

Park takes time out from working on Cobras to play his favorite pinball games. **Phil Berg**

But he's happy with the garage he created when he moved into this location in 1981. Originally, the single-story ranch house, shadowed by the Angeles Crest mountains outside Los Angeles, had just a two-car garage behind it. Right away, Park began expanding the garage.

"We pushed it back as far as we could. We had to have another row of cars. Then we pushed it to the side to do the really dirty work." One side of the garage has a game room, with pinball machines lining one wall, as well as an office and a bathroom. An addition grew soon

after, to house machine tools and cars undergoing complete restoration and modifications.

"My wife and I play the pinball games all the time, and she likes being out here. This is just a good hangout," says Park. "Neighbors have people over, and they just want to come and see the cars. One of my neighbors used the garage as a backdrop to take pictures for their Christmas cards."

When he's not entertaining in the garage, Park works on his cars. "I never get a car that I just leave alone. The first thing I do when I get a car is tear it apart. I make it into my car. That's my big deal. I want something to be *my car*. I buy stuff that other people joke about its condition. I like stuff like that. If you buy something that's already done, it's someone else's car."

Inside, the back walls are lined with antique barn wood Park recovered in 1975 from a barn belonging to a friend in Colorado. "I didn't know what I was going to do with the wood then. When we moved here, I knew what I was going to do with it."

To add 10 or so spaces to his garage, Park had to get a permit from the local municipality. "They said I could do what I wanted but that they didn't want me to make it into living quarters. I was first going to do this without a permit, but I went and got a permit. No sooner than I started the roof, my neighbors started complaining. So I'm glad I got a permit.

"I built the tall ceiling and access to the attic to accommodate the lift," Park explains. Since the attic is the size of a large room, Park was going to turn it into the game room so it could house his collection of pinball games. "But with this ladder and no room for a staircase, we thought somebody would fall down, so it became strictly storage."

The buffalo head hanging above his car collection came from another neighbor. "I put it up there to show 'this is America.' "

Park built all the workbenches and shelves and cabinets himself. "I did the inside, all the barn wood. I just like stuff, memorabilia. I have a friend who has got a nice garage, but it's so sterile—it's block wall and just white and everything is under covers. If he says, 'Look at my collection,' he pulls out a drawer, and when you're finished looking at it, he slides the drawer back in, and that's the end of it. I'm putting my stuff out for everyone to see." When Park was in the military in the late 1960s, he spent a few years overseas and began to collect currency, which is displayed under glass on his workbenches.

Park retired from the elevator business in 1997 and now sells wheels for Cobras. The polished aluminum wheels look so good that some customers use them as furniture. Three wheels stacked up make a bar stool, and one wheel with a glass top makes a coffee table. "The replica Cobra guys love 'em. I've developed a little adapter that allows you to put the Cobra knock-off wheel on a five-lug spindle. I've got a 1956 Ford pickup, and I've got the wheels on that truck."

Park was a Ford hot rod fan in the early 1960s. He recalls that his sister's boyfriend, who was a sports car fan, showed him a copy of *Road & Track* with a photo of Carroll Shelby's new Ford-powered Cobra on the cover. "I went down to the local Ford dealer right away. I thought it was the most amazing thing," Park recalls.

"I couldn't afford a Cobra, so I bought an AC that had a blown Bristol motor and put a Ford motor in it myself. From that point on, 1962, I was a Cobra fanatic, and I have never wavered. I have owned a Porsche or two, but they never kept my interest long enough. I just love Cobras. I race them, I work on them, I sell parts for them, I find them for friends."

Park drives his Cobras a lot. "We just got back from a four-day, 1,400-mile trip from Sun Valley, Idaho, just a group of us that have been doing this for 15 years. There were 14 cars, 14 couples. The first day it was raining. If it rains, you keep going. None of us had rain gear or tops. It was chilly, but you just go. Driving the yellow car, where the exhaust comes out the back, is a piece of cake compared to driving the red one, where the side exhaust is right in your ear."

This trip was unique, Park says, because it was the first time he'd ever been scared while in his Cobra. The group of 14 Cobras was driving down an empty two-lane

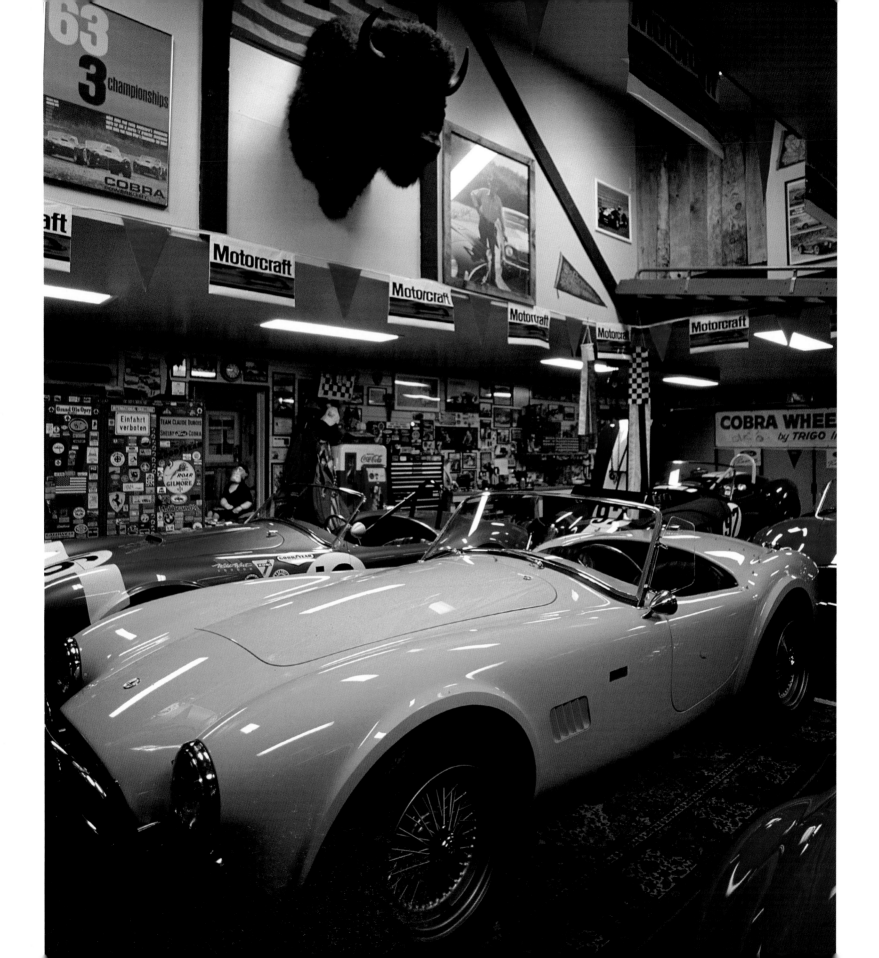

road in Montana. They slowed when the road was suddenly covered with cattle dung. "It was still wet, green, and slimy," he recalls. Farther up the road, "nobody was around except a few cowboys on horses and 300 head of cattle in the middle of the road." One cowboy told the group to follow his horse and not to let a cow get between the horse and the cars.

"We were driving along at a half mile per hour, and this cow gets in between us, and we had to stop, and we lost track of the guy in front. We were surrounded by these giant slobbering cows looking in at us, and they're way up there, and you're thinking, 'What if one of these guys gets spooked and just runs into the car or jumps in the cockpit?' When they're standing right next to you and the snout of the horse is three feet above your head, you think, 'These guys are huge.' " Luckily, there were no Cobra-cow incidents. "The cowboys didn't have a clue what a Cobra was," Park remembers.

"The first thing anyone says when they ask about one of these cars is, 'Is it real or a copy?' I don't really mind—maybe if there get to be enough kit cars and copies, the price will come down on the real Cobras, and I can buy a few more. My beef with the replicas is that they'll call one a 1965 Cobra when it was built in 1992.

"It's easy for me to say that because I've got a lot of Cobras. If I were 20 years younger and couldn't afford $300,000 and I wanted the feel of a Cobra, I'd go buy a replica. I've been very lucky to have gotten them when they were cheap and to have been involved since day one. I've known Carroll Shelby very well for 25 years. I'm just very fortunate. It's the best car that there is."

In the restoration part of the garage, two cars await major work. "I never have time to be bored. You own a car and it's something that always has to be worked on,"

Park operates a wheel-making business from an office at the front of the garage. Cobra owners covet his wheels. Phil Berg

The restoration shop also houses some antique tools that Park has collected. **Phil Berg**

says Park. One car is a 1963 Cobra that Park bought from a Stanford rocket scientist who worked on the Mars lander project. The scientist drove the car from 1963 until 1969, when he was driving up his steep driveway and knocked off the muffler on the curb. He parked the car and let it sit for 32 years. "He didn't cover it; he didn't wipe it off. Then last year he sold it to me," explains Park.

What interested Park most was that the owner had all the original paperwork and letters to Shelby. "This guy didn't like the Lucas wiring, and even though everything worked, he just didn't like it. So he added his own

Left: All Park's Cobras are kept running, and he chooses a different one to drive daily. Phil Berg

switches for the horn and blinker. He converted the generator to an alternator. Every time something was updated at the factory, he would buy that part and put it in." The most notable owner upgrades, however, were shoulder-strap adjusters that came from an air force fighter jet.

Keeping nine Cobras licensed and in running condition doesn't daunt Park. "I don't charge batteries. I just drive the cars," he explains. His favorite road starts a couple blocks from his driveway. "There's no road better than Angeles Crest. Once a month, a whole bunch of us meet here for breakfast, then we drive over the hill. We don't go fast. If you don't go fast, you don't have to pass a bunch of cars and you've got the road to yourselves, and it's a blast. I just love it here."

15

Buddy Pepp

Portrait of a Car Family

There's nothing greater than a wife who helps make your garage look great

Raised next to a Union Oil gas station in California, Buddy Pepp was drawn to the three things that got steady, focused attention at the station: the 1932 Ford hot rods belonging to the station's owner, manager, and assistant manager. Pepp became a child of America's car culture in the constant presence of these cars' modified flathead V-8s.

Today he has a rule about the nine cars he owns: "They all have to be able to go 75 miles per hour on the freeway." That's the only requirement for the eclectic group of machines, unbounded by any period or class. "Well, the fire truck won't go on the freeway," he admits.

He's loved every one of the special cars he's owned, but until 1990 he had no clean and tidy place to put them. "I'd always had this burning desire to have this big garage," says Pepp. By this time he'd become a successful fire hose manufacturer (which explains the fire truck), and his wife, Arline, came up with a plan for a home for the cars. The 10-car garage she designed included massive steel beams, to eliminate having posts holding up the ceiling, and a 900-square-foot guesthouse above.

"We bought our house in 1970," says Pepp. "I went 20 years with a two-car garage that was built in 1927. It had barn doors on it, and it was literally falling apart." Pepp remembers the construction of the new garage and guesthouse as a relatively easy project and has only one regret: "I wish I had plumbed air lines in the walls.

Previous page: The garage is two cars deep, but Buddy Pepp wanted to be able to take a car out of the garage without moving any others. Behind the wooden beams are steel beams holding up the roof and guesthouse. Phil Berg

Pepp's immaculate eight-car garage has two large doors and a spotless tile floor. Phil Berg

It's no big deal—when I have to use air, I drag a hose around the garage. But when you've got the air compressor and have all those walls exposed, it's so easy to run air outlets."

Pepp keeps the garage spotless and talks about it with a warm smile. "I love the fact that I have plenty of storage, a wonderful workbench, great lighting, a desk I can keep all my books and records, and a great tool closet. We really thought it all out pretty well, considering the fact we don't have a lot of space."

The 40-foot-long ceiling beams are covered with wood, and a large skylight along one wall adds daylight when the doors are closed. A custom 36-foot-wide door opens to the alley. A slightly narrower door opens onto

The fire truck rarely moves because it's difficult to maneuver into the alley. Neighborhood children are allowed to play on it in the garage. Phil Berg

Arline Pepp commissioned this large mural, which depicts the couple's first cars and auto-related landmarks. Phil Berg

the driveway to the street in front. Because it has no center posts, with both doors open, the garage feels larger than it is, like an empty airplane hangar.

The guesthouse is slightly smaller than the garage, a result of local building codes. "Adding a guesthouse is cheap, if you think about it, because you're building the foundation, and all you have to do is go up."

Sundays are Pepp's favorite time in the garage. "I probably will spend six to eight hours in the garage

Sunday afternoon. I have battery disconnect switches in every car, and I fire them all up once a month and drive one at least once a week. When it's a Sunday and the weather is nasty, I fire them up just to do it."

Ironically, the cars may not be the biggest attraction. "The garage is kind of neat and the cars in it are kind of neat, but the thing that draws most people, especially people who aren't passionate about cars, is the mural. There's no question," says Pepp.

A red Thunderbird is one of the cars featured in the Pepps' mural. Phil Berg

The mural depicts all the cars Pepp has owned. "There's a 1958 Studebaker Golden Hawk, an Austin Healy, a '57 T-bird, there's a 1950 Ford, a '65 Mustang convertible, and a '62 Corvette. I think the only car in that mural that I still own is the Corvette—and that mural was done in 1990. So since that time, '90 to present, I've sold all those cars and I've replaced them with others. Very fondly, I can remember them all."

The fuel station in the mural is based on one Pepp grew up next to. The colonial house is his house today, and the image of the Holiday Inn is a reproduction from a photo of the first example of the motel chain in Memphis. The Art Deco diner is an artist's conception and is named after Pepp's wife.

"My wife had the mural in mind when we built the garage with the sky windows." Pepp explains. "That mural was my fiftieth birthday present." Arline Pepp found an artist and brainstormed about a collage that would depict memorable moments in their lives. The artist made many preliminary sketches for the mural. "The final product was about idea number 12 or 13," recalls Pepp. "We went through a lot before we finally combined a whole bunch of ideas into this one."

Once a men's magazine heard about Pepp's garage and thought it looked good enough for a photo shoot. "They were willing to pay big bucks, and I said. 'No problem at all.' Then I told my wife they would have some naked ladies there, and she said, 'Not on your life.' "

The one vehicle in the garage that Pepp doesn't drive regularly is a 1922 Model T fire truck, manufactured by Howe fire apparatus. "I was in the fire hose manufacturing business from 1962 to 1992, and during that period of time we would go exhibit our products at various conventions." In the 1970s, Pepp's company bought the fire truck to promote its hoses.

Collections of antique tire repair kits are displayed on the walls. Phil Berg

"It was all original, built in Waverly, Illinois. It had every accessory on it from 1922, and we bought it and had it restored. It runs. It's great, but to be candid with you, it doesn't move. Between my grandchildren and the children in the neighborhood and friends and family, they just climb all over it and ring the bell and have a good time in the garage—that's why it's there. It's capable of running, but it's a pain in the ass to get it in and out of the alley. So it's more fun just to leave it alone."

Pepp is an example of a car nut who inherited his enthusiasm. "My father was passionate about European touring cars. He had an Iso Rivolta, a Facel Vega, and he enjoyed their performance and that type of thing." Pepp says this inspired his love of Ferraris and the Pantera he owns. "By osmosis, I guess, I had the urge to have some high-performance fun cars. There has been one Ferrari in my life that I've always found stunning, and I've always loved the Dino more than any other body style. I've craved others, but this one you can drive anywhere. And the Panteras I think are fun, fun, fun, and mine happens to be dead stock. Out of every 200 Panteras, you'll find one stock."

Nevertheless, the influence of the 1932 Ford hot rods from the Union Oil station runs deep. "In the last 10 years, I've probably driven the street rods more than I have the Italian cars," he admits.

Pepp's tools are hidden in a locker, but on display are Monkey Grip tire-patch kits and glass ashtrays wrapped with small tires. "I enjoy going to swap meets and am a collector of tire ashtrays and tube-patch kits. I have well in excess of a hundred each. I somehow started collecting them, and the more I collected them, the more I learned about them and the more interested I became. It just became a fun thing to collect, and they're relatively plentiful. They're nice—it's a fun thing to do."

This sign differentiates the garage entrance from the door to the guesthouse. **Phil Berg**

The garage was built just before local codes were changed to increase restrictions on setbacks and guesthouses. **Phil Berg**

Pepp is content to keep his collection at 10 vehicles and not only because that's all the space he has. "There are a lot of other cars I really enjoy and would love to have, but to be honest, I'm not enjoying to the fullest extent the cars I have. That's because there's just not enough hours in the week. I work full time, we travel all the time, I have kids and grandchildren. If I bought more cars, I'd have to ignore the ones I have. And I absolutely adore the ones I have. I absolutely love them. The ones I was halfway in love with, the '65 Mustang and the '57 T-bird and the '58 Studebaker Golden Hawk, I sold because I found something that got my excitement to a higher level.

"We're really happy with the place. It gives us a lot of joy. I hope to be in that garage for another 25 years if the good Lord gives me good health."

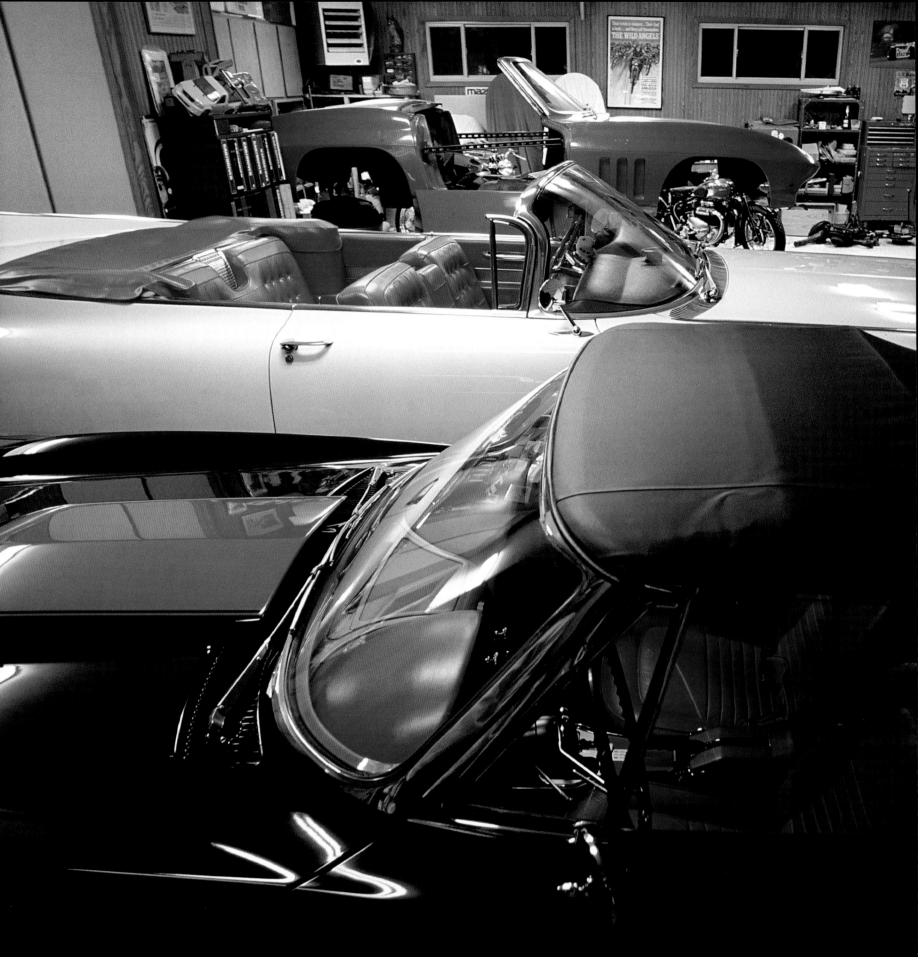

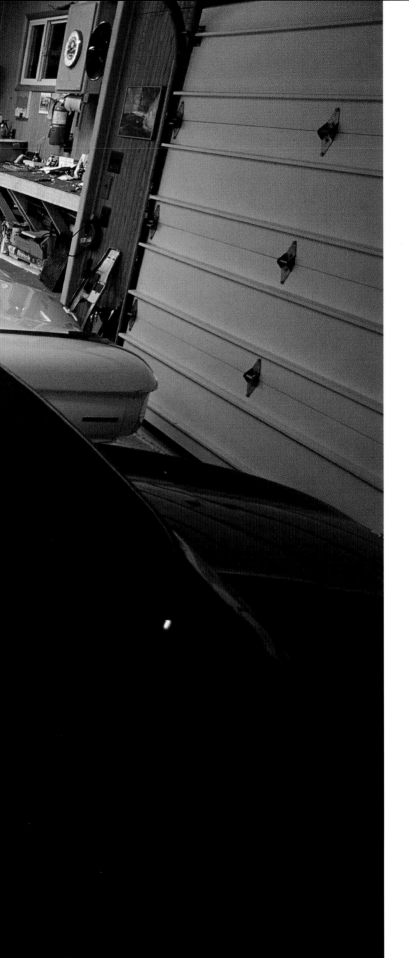

16

Don Sherman

Hobby Meets Business

A car tester needs
room to learn the art
of restoration

Before he built his garage, Don Sherman devoted almost all his time to his day job: editor and technical editor of *Car and Driver*. But when he decided to work at home in 1988, he was eager to keep busy.

Sherman is a hands-on guy who made a reputation at *Car and Driver* for always making what he needed to test cars and for taking them apart to find out how they worked or had broken. The 54-year-old car tester is a tool user as well as a journalist and engineer.

His boomerang-shaped, 1962 bi-level house built on a small bluff on a peninsula jutting into Belleville Lake,

Previous page: In the foreground is Don Sherman's original two-car garage, with his Sting Ray and Cadillac convertible. He restored both after building the addition. **Phil Berg**

Michigan, had a standard 20-by-24-foot two-car attached garage. He bought the house in 1981, but the big change came in 1988, when he got married, began working at home, and, just before the birth of his first son, was infected with a bug to restore cars. "It became clear that I needed more room," he says.

Many of Sherman's projects last late into the evening, including his magazine and book writing, which he does in the office above the garage. **Phil Berg**

He planned to add 20 more feet on the end of the house and expand the depth of the new, bigger garage to 28 feet. Above this he planned a 30-by-15-foot office and an attached powder room. "The inspector didn't see this," adds Sherman, noting that adding the bathroom would qualify the office as living space and raise his taxes.

Back downstairs in the garage, he decided not to install a second two-car garage door on the addition, simply because it would have made the angled house look disproportionately garage-dominated from the street. Besides, the addition was a place to work on cars and motorcycles, not space for commuter cars. Even with the addition, Sherman's commuter cars stay outside in the weather.

Where the second garage door might have gone, Sherman built his own workbench, a 16-foot-long plywood counter that's "as deep as a carpet runner from Home Depot. That way, when it gets greasy, you just get another runner." Another explanation: "Benches that are deeper, you get a bunch of stuff on the back, and it ends up being clutter."

Sherman raised the rear half of the garage roof so that the pitch of the front remained untouched. The roof's pitch on the new second story is perpendicular to the pitch of the rest of the roof, and the pitches are asymmetrical. Sherman likes the fact that the different pitches allow the most space under a roof that intrudes the least above the original house.

The size of the garage was determined by a ratio of price and maximum realistic size. The price started to climb exponentially when interior spans exceeded 20 feet. Instead of having posts inside the garage holding up roof trusses, Sherman chose three interconnected steel beams supported by steel four-by-four posts set in the perimeter. That way, there's nothing for him to hit when he's moving cars around inside.

Brick pavers replaced the original concrete driveway after the garage was built, extending the driveway to a parking area that will hold three cars. Total parking room is now six cars and three motorcycles, but the cul de sac handles overflow.

A former neighbor of Sherman's, an architect who had his own construction company and had built a carriage house for another neighbor, built the addition. "What he brought to the party was how much it cost and what it would take to make it look acceptable," says Sherman. "All I was after was space. He blended a house into an acceptable garage space."

The garage addition wasn't finished right away—the office had priority. "We told the contractor to hurry up. We didn't need the construction mess in the house. We were having a baby." Four to five months after the framing, the concrete floor was poured for the garage and the walls were paneled. Even so, he had his first son on the way and didn't have time to do any of the remodeling himself. It was done in stages, first completing the shell, and then finishing the inside as the family's needs allowed.

"Every three or four years this garage is pristine," he says, but he points to the current stains and dirt as badges of accomplishment. "I take everything out, clean it, and paint the floor and put in new carpet." The floor gets epoxy paint, but he prefers thin carpet as a working surface instead of the concrete or metal you'll find in most shops. A typical good-weather day means the garage door is always open, so dust and dirt and bugs find their way inside. He's considering installing a sump to catch fluids, but otherwise the floor has no drain.

Sherman briefly considered an off-site office but quickly rejected the idea because his work is so closely tied to the cars in his garage and his driveway, which include preproduction magazine test cars. "I like being home because the boys are here, and I can play with them when I want."

Inside the garage is a 1979 RX-7, unrestored but clean and sentimental, since Sherman bought it new. It

A body rack Sherman built to restore Corvettes allows the car to be moved to make space for other projects. The latest project is revamping a rare four-cylinder Ariel motorcycle. Phil Berg

now has 22,000 miles on it. Next to it is a 1967 Corvette, and angled into the doorless addition is a 1960 Cadillac convertible.

He picked the Cadillac as his first restoration project in 1989. "The prospect of the job was not planned nor feared," he says. Sherman can't decide whether he planned the garage addition to be 20 feet long because somewhere in his mind he had the idea of getting a gargantuan Cadillac to restore or whether he bought the Cadillac because that's the biggest car that would fit in his new addition. He figures it's the karma of

making the garage look right that resulted in the adequate space.

The Cadillac was stripped to the frame from its cowl forward, then the rear body was taken down to just the metal. He hauled the body of the Cadillac around the Detroit area on a trailer to get bids for bodywork and paint. "I got a shockingly high bid in Waterford," he explains. "That's when I knew that's where I wanted to take the car." He left the car there for most of a year, where the rust was stripped and panels straightened. In 1993, he took it to the Meadowbrook concours show.

Sherman assembles new parts for his latest Corvette restoration on the carpet before assembly. **Phil Berg**

The Corvette was next, in 1994. "It's typical that before one project is finished, you start the next one," he explains. So as the Cadillac was winding to a close, he started looking for another ragtop. "The Corvette is smaller and has less upholstery than the Cadillac. It had to be less work, I thought.

"When I bought the car, it had the wrong wheels and tires, the fenders had flares, and there was a duck-tail spoiler. It was a 50-50 mix of shitty and excellent. None of the original driveline was there. It wasn't even a runner. It wouldn't drive for more than a few miles." The car came from a friend, who had bought it new. Sometime in the 1980s he had replaced the frame, which had rusted away in the salty Michigan winters. The second frame also was shot, and Sherman replaced it.

"The good part was [that] it was a three-carb 427 and was drag-raced most of its life. Holes had been punched in the floor whenever U-joints broke. The engine had been blown several times." But he got it for a low price, the mileage was low, and it had no parking lot dings or traffic dents.

"Restoration is not a business or an investment but a hobby," he says. "Look at what happened with Ferrari prices in the late 1980s. You always put more into them than you can sell them for. You can't restore anything for less than $35,000."

Sherman's cars get less than 1,000 miles per year because he doesn't want to use them too much and wind up having to restore them all over again.

Because the garage won't hold any more cars, he switched to restoring motorcycles. Out of a barn in Coldwater, Michigan, he bought a 1971 Triumph in 1996 and dragged it home as a warmup project. "I was

interested in motorcycles, and they would fit in the garage," he says.

"I wanted to improve the Triumph, bob it, or customize it. I wanted to strip off the ugly things, like the turn signals, and make it look better. The seat was ugly. The new one is narrower and shorter but only about halfway to what it needs to be. The handlebars are too wide and comfy—they need to be halfway to a clip-on style from where I'm at now."

In 1999, he found an unrestored 1939 Ariel square-four motorcycle and spent three years restoring it to show quality. "It's utter perfection," he says. All the skills he learned with the cars and the Triumph have been brought to bear on the Ariel, including the use of stainless fasteners. He won two trophies in 2002 and has the widest smile when he can start the engine with just four kicks. It idles like a new Honda, which is a trick for a square-four that has manual timing and mixture-adjustment levers on the handlebars.

"I want to enjoy what I do. The cars are best driven at night in the summer with the top down. They are just in their element then. I have never driven them at night when I didn't come home with a smile," he says. "My ultimate goal is not to give them away or sell them. But if I need to liquidate to pay for college for the boys, then they're here. With these cars, I learned how to make money, too. I wrote a book about the Corvette restoration—sold stories, too. I had a lot of time on my hands, and I wanted to stay home."

His final philosophy: "The most fun you ever have is the next project."

17

Tom Sparks

Studio Collection

You've probably
seen one of
these cars on
the big screen

Of the hundreds of one-of-a-kind classic cars Tom Sparks has owned and restored and been the nanny for, no single car stands out. "Cars are like children—you can't have favorites," he explains. So the long-time hobbyist and craftsman has a "family" of 25 special cars he keeps in a loosely tied-together group of structures behind his modest Hollywood Hills bungalow.

Not many car enthusiasts can get away with packing their homes with the hundreds of models and trinkets of car enthusiasm as Sparks does in every room in his home, which gives you an idea of the esteem in which he's held by his human family. Soft-spoken and in his 70s, Sparks' eyes twinkle with interest even when he uses them to give a once-over to a hotted-up Nissan SE-R kid's car.

If you ask Tom Sparks how much time he spends in his garage, he answers, "I go out there about once every three months to start the cars, or when I have to get a car out."

Ask his wife, Laura, however, and she says, "He's out there every day."

Sparks is known by two industries in which he's excelled. One was restoring classic cars to such high standards that he has a wall full of photos of Pebble Beach concours winners he's brought back to life. The other was loaning cars to the movie industry.

"I once had a Maserati Grand Prix car that [Juan Manuel] Fangio originally drove, and then it was used in a movie called *The Racers* with Kirk Douglas." During the filming of the 1955 movie, the car had been crashed and

Previous page: From his original collection of 100 cars, Tom Sparks decided to keep 25, including this Model T hot rod. It sits between the two larger structures that make up his garage. Phil Berg

The rest of Sparks' cars reside in the garage compound behind his house. Phil Berg

Sparks starts and runs each car periodically, to keep the batteries charged and just to hear how they run. Phil Berg

burned for a scene. The production company was going to send the remains to a junkyard. "I said at least let me haul it away," Sparks recalls. "I hauled it home and restored it and ran it in a couple of races."

Sparks makes this sound like easy work, an understandable result of reflecting on more than 50 years of car tinkering, collecting, and racing. He remembers this, however: "I was so broke. Every penny I made was going

into nitromethane and alcohol for the drag cars, and I thought, 'I've got to start doing something that makes money.' " So by 1960, he began making parts for classic cars, rebuilding the cars, and then collecting them.

By 1987, Sparks' car rental business for the movie studios had been booming for 20 years, making him an easy choice to supply cars for *Tucker*. "I worked on the *Tucker* movie for a little over a year," he recalls of the film.

Sparks continues to restore, fix, and tinker with his cars in the shop. Phil Berg

Sparks was tasked with finding 24 Tucker Torpedos. Only 51 of the cars were built, all in 1948. "I did all the original Tuckers for the movie," he recalls. "Plus I built five replicas, and I built the crash car."

More difficult was getting them to run reliably. "Tucker originally used a 496-cubic-inch flat six-cylinder that did not use a cam—it used timed oil injection to work the valves. And it never worked. Never ran for more than a few seconds."

Director Francis Ford Coppola first told Sparks he wanted a chassis without a body for the assembly-line scene in the movie. The only chassis Sparks could find was an engine cradle in New York, which he was planning to have shipped to him.

"Then Coppola said, 'Well I want to see these cars doing figure-eights out in front of this set.' I told him, 'Hey, I'm going to rig it so it'll go back and forth on cables—the car don't run.' He said, 'Well then, make it run.' I said, 'That ain't going to happen.' He said, 'That's what we hired you for. It's your duty.' So I built a fake sheet-metal engine and stuck a Corvair engine inside of it."

With barely 100 horsepower pushing them, the heavy Tucker cars weren't fast, but they worked reliably for the movie, which premiered in 1988.

When Sparks started restoring classics in the 1960s, he immersed himself in Duesenbergs. "I've restored four of them, so I know who you gotta know to get anything. Everything is available. It's just knowing who has it. I learned how to make body panels, everything mechanical. There are more Duesenberg roadsters today than the company ever produced."

There are no Tuckers or Duesenbergs in Sparks' garage today. He bought the house and garage in 1976 because he knew the owner, who restored brass-era classic cars in the garage. In fact, the garage can be described as three or four garages tied together by different roofs. The main portion of the garage holds perhaps 16 cars cheek to jowl, with barely enough space for a person to tiptoe around.

What looks like a two-car garage with two single-car garages added single-file behind it is connected to the main garage by a covered terrace, under which is Sparks' first hot rod—a 1917 Model T pickup that he bought in 1942. "I painted it 25 years ago because until then it was just primer. I bought a pickup because it was available and it was cheap. Cars cost $25 then."

Dozens of teardrop spotlights and old headlight assemblies hang from the ceiling of the main garage, and almost every square inch of wall is covered by a poster or sign. At one time in his career he rented the memorabilia to the movies, too. Between his house and the main garage is a one-room office that contains neatly arranged machine tools left over from his former shop. He opened it in 1952, across the street from Paramount studios, and closed it when he retired in 1997. "I had 100 cars there once," he recalls. "The first

few years it was hot rods and sports cars because sports cars like MGs were getting popular."

Sparks' garage holds three Pierce-Arrows now, but one is an 1895 bicycle—a shaft-drive model produced before the company got into cars. It reminds Sparks of when he started racing bicycles in 1958.

When Sparks moved out of the shop near Paramount, he moved everything to his home garage, and in 2000, he built the office. "I had nice neighbors—nobody ever complained. To get a car out of here, I sometimes have to move a dozen cars. I won't park them on the street. I park them on the front lawn—never for more than a couple hours. The local parking enforcement patrols regularly cruise Sparks' neighborhood, hoping for a quick dozen tickets on the permit-restricted street in front of Sparks' home.

"That's why I closed the shop up. I got tired of all the local parking rules and regulations. They make it hard on you."

Sparks doesn't know the age of his garage structures, but they've survived several severe earthquakes. After the Northridge earthquake of 1994, five cars had to be repainted. They were parked close enough together that they bumped each other as they bounced during the quake. "You see that crease there?" Sparks asks, pointing to a 1953 Buick Skymaster convertible. "I worked it out as good as I could without hurting the paint. Five of them I had to repaint, but this one I couldn't."

When Sparks sold his shop near Paramount, he had to cut down from more than a hundred classics to his current group of 25 cars. "I got rid of the nondescript cars that would sit in the background on a movie set and that I didn't pay much for. I kept the ones that I couldn't easily get cheap from somebody else. Studios always came to me and a dozen other guys to get the cars, and maybe 15 years ago, somebody got the bright idea of buying up all the cars. When it was one guy it was OK, but now it's like 30 guys, and they're all cutting prices."

The only problem with parking the cars this close is that several had to be repainted after bumping each other during an earthquake. Phil Berg

What he kept was a 1940 Lincoln Continental, which was a model produced before they were called that. The car is one of 30 that Edsel Ford designed in 1937 for his trips to Palm Springs. Thirty were built with 12-cylinder engines, and they eventually went into production in 1941, which explains the Zephyr labels on the radio and hubcaps.

Next to it is a 1935 Pierce-Arrow, a 1932 Studebaker President, a 1940 Packard, a 1925 Pierce-Arrow roadster, a 1935 Desoto, a 1941 Plymouth Woody, a 1966 Chevy Belair, a 1955 Jaguar XK140, a 1938 Packard Town Car, a 1936 Ford, a 1968 Mercedes, a 1979 Ferrari 308, a 1935 12-cylinder Cadillac, and a 1956 Thunderbird.

The front building, the original two-car garage, holds a 1938 Cord that Sparks' wife bought new. They use it as a family car. "Nobody's ever laid a wrench on it but me," says Sparks. "The Ferrari usually sits where the Cord is now, but one of the cars I've got out at the movies right now is a 1929 Packard Dual Cowl Phaeton, which usually sits where the Ferrari is," he explains.

All of the cars in Sparks' garage are licensed and insured. "That's kind of stupid because there's no reason to license them, except I've just always done it. Almost everyone else who does this has a dealer's license, and maybe that's what I should have done."

Sparks says the Ferrari and the Model T hot rod are his favorite street cars, and he drives them a lot. "I don't enjoy

Sparks' wife, Laura, bought this Cord new in 1938. Sparks takes pride in being the only person who has ever worked on it. **Phil Berg**

Behind the MG (storing a Corvette hardtop) is an enormous collection of old magazines and books about cars. Phil Berg

driving the others because I know if something breaks, I gotta fix it, and I don't enjoy people staring and swerving and getting too damn close to you, and you can't park them anyplace. I like to talk to them and look at them. You don't have to drive old cars to enjoy old cars.

"I go on a hot rod run every year. Old car tours I don't do anymore, but I belong to all the clubs, and I could go on one every two weekends." The hot rod reached 114 miles per hour in 1946, which is not bad for a $25 car.

These days, Sparks isn't looking for more cars. "I haven't bought a car in nine years. I outgrew that. I'm happy to be here now and take care of what I got."

18

Dean Stanley

Cozy Quarters for Cars

Techniques
learned in Tokyo
make this garage
a space saver

The two years Dean Stanley spent in Tokyo had a profound impact on the garage he built eight years later in the United States. His Michigan bungalow nestles in a quaint old suburb with charming custom 1930s homes on tiny 40-foot lots. Stanley needed the biggest garage he could squeeze behind his house while not breaching local setback and height codes. He also needed a home office/workshop and a place to plan a thorough remodeling of his two-story home.

After consulting an architect and studying framing manuals, Stanley came up with a plan for an L-shaped structure that measured 600 square feet just four feet behind his house. The clever design holds four cars and lets him pursue his tinkering hobbies on three spacious workbenches. The garage comes within two feet of his neighbors' backyards and leaves only enough room in the yard between it and his house for a small patio. But that's exactly the way he and his wife like it.

The end result is an optical illusion. From the street, the garage looks only slightly larger than the small two-car garages squeezed behind other homes in the area. Stanley's garage adds a small wing off to the left, which holds the lift. The wing also has an access door that opens at the end, but not onto a driveway—it's merely for light and some elbow room as Stanley fills shelves with tools and spare parts. The Tokyo influence is seen in

Previous page: Dean Stanley laid the brick patio outside his garage himself. Like everything else in the garage, the old gas pump is mounted on casters, so it can be rolled where needed for atmosphere. Phil Berg

The white MR2 under restoration resides on the lift. The Toyota-powered Lotus replica lives under it most of the time. Phil Berg

Shelves built into the wall of the office/workshop on the second floor leave space for lounge chairs.
An inspector told Stanley that the permanent stairs classify this area as living space. **Phil Berg**

every inch: No space is wasted. Shelves line the walls up to the 15-foot-high ceiling, and cabinets are squeezed under stairs and into attic spaces. Stanley has to climb on his lift to reach the top shelves.

Inside, the garage holds three Toyota MR2 coupes and a custom-built replica of a Caterham Super Seven roadster, itself a copy of a Lotus Super Seven. It's an odd collection, but the cars have a logical connection. The

meticulously fabricated Super Seven has been converted to Toyota twin-cam 1.6-liter power, the same engine you'll find in each of the MR2 coupes.

Stanley experiments with valve timing and carburetion and other hot rod tricks on the Toyota motors. One of the MR2s is a parts car, one is a clean commuter car, and one is a tourer that has seen a few cross-country banzai runs and is awaiting restoration. A fourth MR2 winter beater sits outside, rusty but reliable, in anticipation of utility duty. Measuring just 14 feet long, the speedy little Toyotas will fit where other cars won't.

Stanley, a 42-year-old quality control specialist at a large automaker supply company, spends his early Sunday mornings in the Super Seven, driving rural back roads. He hones his skills on racetracks during club events, too. He's also taken the long-distance-outfitted MR2 on cross-continental drives, creating his own mini–Cannonball Run.

Upstairs is the workshop with shelving and files to store magazine articles, models, memorabilia, and projects. The drill press and a welding station flank the large wraparound workbench, which is covered with linoleum so that gas dripping from Weber carburetors in the middle of a rebuild won't stain the surface. The upstairs floor is tiled in vinyl, and the downstairs floor is cement painted with epoxy.

Across from the workbench upstairs sits a drafting table, on which plans were hatched for car-part fabrication and the pending house remodeling job. The ceiling of the second-floor workshop is seven and a half feet high at the ridge, sloping down to five and a half feet high at

The only access from the street is through the double-door driveway, which widens from 10 feet as it passes the house. Phil Berg

the walls. The parking spaces below the second-floor workshop have seven-foot-high ceilings, and a Chevy Astro van will fit here as well as it would in a normal garage. The total height of the garage is just 15 feet, the maximum allowed by the neighborhood zoning.

The second floor of the garage was added after the outside structure had been built and inspected. But when the inspector saw the addition, he gave it his stamp of approval. The upstairs workshop feels surprisingly roomy, even with the compact ceilings. "I think I'd feel claustrophobic if the ceiling was only six feet high," he says.

Just because the second floor was built as an add-on doesn't mean it's flimsy. A 10-inch steel beam on four-inch-square steel posts supports the workshop over the two-car space below, which is notable overkill. It's just the beginning of the overdesign that makes this small garage feel sturdier than a bomb shelter. Posts and rafters have been doubled and tripled everywhere on the exposed framing, and large eye bolts with hooks hang everywhere in case a heavy engine or transmission needs to be hoisted.

The side wing of the garage was left open to the rafters inside, to make room for a lift. Windows on the side and end of the wing let light in during the day, and every inch of the ceiling ridge beam has either tube lights or incandescent bulb fixtures. At one end of the second floor is a balcony with a half-high wall that's open to the lift. This lets Stanley work on a car on the lift, while another car remains parked below.

The interior walls are covered with plywood instead of drywall and are painted semigloss white. This makes the space look larger than it is and keeps a lot of light inside. The plywood and painted framing suit Stanley, who likes to tack up memorabilia, photos, and tools wherever is handy at the moment.

The space does not appear unfinished, as you might expect it to. One reason for this becomes obvious if you inspect the joints where framing and plywood meet. They're caulked so well that you'd think the entire garage could be filled with water without leaking a drop.

More elements of the overdesign—as evident as the proliferation of electrical outlets—are the hurricane ties used on all the framing pieces, about four times as many as required by code. It's not complete whimsy, however, since Michigan averages one significant tornado each year.

Heat is provided by a single gas blower in the ceiling of the wing. Because the garage is in the north, Stanley thoroughly insulated the walls, ceilings, and doors, so even in the middle of winter the place stays warm and cozy.

Intercoms tied into the phone system and three separate, buried conduit channels carry electricity, gas, and communications between the house and garage. The garage has at least 80 electrical outlets (Stanley's never counted), wired through a subpanel separate from the house. A large, rolling generator—a remnant of Y2K preparation—can supply both the house and garage with electricity during a power outage.

Like the generator, every machine tool and cabinet is mounted on large rollers, including the heavy-duty arbor press so that the garage can be rearranged in minutes. It doesn't take long to conclude that with all the lift and hoist attachments, and the outlets with trouble lights hanging everywhere, this is one of the most convenient garages in which to fix car problems.

"I've probably gone way over the price-per-square-foot formula building this place," Stanley says.

That's not including the hours he spent finishing the place himself, rebuilding the interior and adding the second-floor workshop after the first inspections.

Now that Stanley has assembled all the tools he needs, his goal is to build a roadster of his own design, most likely powered by the little Toyota twin-cam and inspired by his secret dream car: a Lancia Stratos. You saw its birthplace here first.

173

Part 3

Non-Traditional Garages

19

Curt Catallo

A Magic Vision for Car Space

A son carries on his father's vision for a sacred place for cars

Before 1980, Clarence Catallo and his wife and kids lived on a farm in rural Michigan that was ideal for a car nut. It had a couple of barns full of cars and parts, with no limit to space. But that fateful year, they saw an abandoned Methodist church in a small town on the fringes of Detroit.

"My parents saw it, and crazy as they were at the time, they thought it would be a great house for them," says Curt Catallo, son of the late creator of the famed little Deuce Coupe. The church had been abandoned in the 1950s, after the congregation built a much larger church down the otherwise residential street, and was full of pigeons. All the windows had been knocked out,

Section opener: Architect Dan Scully built his garage from unassembled Quonset hut materials. Jeff Hackett

Previous page: When not on loan to a museum or at a car show, the Deuce Coupe owned by Curt Catallo resides below a converted Methodist church in Michigan. Jim Frenak

Because the church only had a one-car garage beneath it, Clarence Catallo built a three-car carriage house behind it to hold his favorite cars. Jim Frenak

too. "It was a mess," Curt recalls, but his folks persevered and moved in in 1980. "As is always the case, they probably moved in six months too early."

"My parents have pretty eclectic and eccentric tastes," says Catallo. "It was just a perfect place. I have to give them a lot of credit for designing most of it on cocktail napkins. For a couple of amateurs, they did a very nice job designing that. It's now a three-bedroom house with four full baths. You start with a box, and you build a loft inside it. You modify it accordingly. You're dividing the rooms but not adding ceilings, so it will still have high ceilings."

Originally, the church had a one-car garage built into in the back at street level, "probably something that existed so that they could put tables for banquets into the lower level," says Catallo. (The main level, now the living quarters, is one story up.) This area is the current home to the Deuce Coupe, but for a car guy it's not enough room. So just three years after the Catallos bought the church, they built a three-car carriage house behind it, to store some of Clarence Catallo's dozen cars. "Their plan was to use the upstairs of the carriage house as guest quarters," Curt remembers. "But it quickly filled with car parts and stuff. It has parts for cars we sold long ago."

The carriage house matched the look of the church. "It was very important to them to create a structure that was historically appropriate. They created a very traditional carriage house with a footprint that my dad could maximize, so he could fit as many cars and toys in there as possible," Curt recalls.

"My dad was a man who was addicted to dollies. He bought whatever was advertised in *Hemmings*, *Griot's*, and that. He would buy all different types of dollies, in an attempt to fit as many vehicles in as confined a space as possible." Moving from the country to a small town meant using any means to make up for giving up all of the pole barns and space. "That was the real hit, moving from the country to the city. If you had a bunch

It was important to the Catallos that the carriage house's architecture reflected the historic look of their small town neighborhood. **Jim Frenak**

of cars and projects, you couldn't keep them. We're still spread around."

The Catallos tried using space off-site at a nearby airport. "He had hangars and was a hot-air pilot. He put a balloon in each hangar, so he could register an N number with the county. We had friends who had hang gliders hanging in our hangars, so you could say there was an aircraft in there and store more cars."

Clarence Catallo's car passion began in Ford's hometown. "My dad was just a little hot-rodder from Dearborn. When he was a kid, he bought a '32 Ford at the gas station across the street from his parents'

The inside of the Catallos' carriage house, built in 1983, looks like a normal three-car garage. **Jim Frenak**

grocery store," Curt says. The elder Catallo partnered with the Alexander Brothers, well-known hot rod fabricators, to create the Deuce Coupe. Then he moved to Long Beach, to work at the shop of the even more famous George Barris.

"By then the car hobby was a full-blown obsession," says Curt. "He sold the coupe a couple years later in

1965 and bought himself a new Porsche and married my mom. That was the last of the hot rods, and he became a Porsche freak and returned to Michigan. Along the way, we had some pretty important cars.

"He became a stockbroker, and that worked out because it allowed him to buy more cars. He at one time had a rare 1948 Porsche Gmund coupe, an RS61 Le Mans

One of the reasons the Catallos began collecting motorcycles is because they could fit more of them into the garages than they could cars. The purple Indian in the back belonged to motorcycle fan Steve McQueen. Jim Frenak

Passersby probably do not suspect that car enthusiasts often gather behind this residence. The car buffs are drawn by Mark Donohue's winning Lola T70 racer, famous Porsches, and the Ferrari 375 from the Sophia Loren movie Boy on a Dolphin. Jim Frenak

factory race car, and the Ferrari 375 from the Sophia Loren movie *Boy on a Dolphin.* It was all stuff that he kept in the driveway. He loved cars and loved sharing them. He loved popping the doors open and letting people into them."

Clarence Catallo never did the actual restoration work on his cars himself. Curt recalls, "From the get-go he was smart enough to recognize talent, and whether it was Alexander brothers or Junior Conway out at George Barris' shop, he was smart enough to let the pros do the work. He helped out as he could. He worked at Barris' shop doing grunt work in exchange for a paint job because that was his talent."

The car obsession was obvious at the Catallo household. "My dad had the Mark Donohue Lola T70, the one that he won the championship with Penske in 1966, and he kept that car in the garage at home, and he'd have his Porsche daily driver parked an hour away. He wanted certain cars nearby because he liked to look at them without driving them."

The passion in this case was passed on to son Curt. "Water seeks its own level—the bigger the garage, you'll fill it. Nobody who likes cars should have an empty space. My dad was never disciplined about space. If he had a one-car garage, he'd have six cars. If he had 100-car garage, he'd have 106 cars. He always had a formula: room plus five. If you couldn't find a car, you had to look in the trailer because sometimes he'd hide one in there. When he died in 1998, he was up to space plus 10."

"Toward the end, my dad and I started getting into motorcycles. One of the reasons was that you could fit so many into a small space. It was fun to have a multitude of bikes, where if you had as many cars, you'd need a pole barn. All we've got at home now are the 1965 and 1957 Speedster, a '67 Karmann Ghia, and the coupe lives in there, too. We've got eight or 10 bikes in there right now, including the 1931 Indian Scout of Steve McQueen's, up to my BMW Paris-Dakar."

"I've kind of taken the garage over. It sees a lot of action still," adds Curt, who is following in his dad's renovating footsteps, having bought another church a block away from the first one and turned it into a restaurant. "We're pretty well versed on renovating a church. It's nice because it's traditional, but at the same time, you can do so much with it. The restaurant is just a block away. One of the reasons the structure appealed to us is that we had a background with churches."

Growing up in the midst of special cars and places for them had an effect. "As a kid, I was obsessed with the garage from the TV show *Vegas,*" says Catallo about the 1980s show with a fictional private eye who drove his Thunderbird into the living room/garage of his remodeled warehouse home. "I still wake up in the middle of the night with a smile on my face having dreamed of a place like that."

Living with cars is Curt's passion, too. "I think the farther you are from the cars, the more ridiculous it is to have them. I love it when they're as congruent with your lifestyle as possible," says Catallo. It's the same with guitars: If you have a guitar in its case, you'll rarely play it. If you have it on a stand and you can just grab it when you walk by and goof around for a couple minutes, you'll become a much better player. I think with cars you should always have the keys in, and my dad's thing was sometimes he would decide to go out and get a pizza, and he'd just fire a car up and go do it. I think that's the way you gotta use it, But that's easier said than done.

"The neighbors know that the Catallos have car 'problems,' so they're used to us firing something silly up at 11:30 at night or leaving the tandem-axle trailer out all night on the street. We're very fortunate they roll with the punches because it's not easy living next to car people."

"Without a doubt, my dad's favorite time was showing other car guys his favorite cars," adds Curt. "To him, the coolest thing was just idle car talk, with people who loved silly cars. . . . The only thing he loved more than cars were car people, and he loved sharing it."

183

20

Horsepower TV

Locked Inside For a Week

A studio transforms
into a race team's garage
on a moment's notice

"**T**his is guerilla television," says Don Cadorette, executive producer of two increasingly popular how-to car shows that feature modifying muscle cars and trucks. Cadorette says that these shows, produced in a 9,000-square-foot ex–race car shop, are done on a shoestring. But what's skimpy for TV is overendowed for hard-core gearheads. The facilities that the production company has acquired in the seven years since the shows began are a hot-rodder's dream.

The reality is that Cadorette is living the life portrayed in fiction by comedian Tim Allen on the television show *Home Improvement.* He's making a television show about what he loves to do, which is work on cars. Just about every tool that's possible to use on a car is displayed and available inside the neat, clean shop, with lighting from more than 100 fixtures.

Dream is something Cadorette does well. "We just put in a rolling dynamometer last year. Eventually, I want to put in an engine dyno with bulletproof glass and a paint booth. We'll knock out another wall into the parking lot to do that. Every year, we want to do something new, something different." Tool makers are eager to donate whatever the shop needs, in the hope that their products will appear on the show.

So far, about a million viewers watch the shows on Saturday and Sunday, says Cadorette, who believes one reason for the shows' popularity is that everyone involved loves cars and working on cars. "Everybody gets along great. There's something about car people like that. I don't know what it is."

In 1996, Cadorette reached an agreement with cable TV network TNN to produce a hands-on hot rod car show. The bad news was that he had no car, no host, and eight weeks to come up with the first program.

The first step was to find a place to create the show. Cadorette had hired former *PM Magazine* television host Joe Elmore, who knew a local NASCAR racer who was leaving his shop north of town. It was a metal building

with a concrete floor and very little else. "I hate to admit it was a smart thing to do because I was against buying this shop," recalls Cadorette. "The first year we shot, we slammed the set together in eight weeks—we just shot against two walls."

"The garage was an empty building. If you dropped a wrench, it would go *DING, Ding, ding.*" Cadorette recalls that the wiring was insufficient for the lights and camera equipment they would need. The acoustics were bad, and the walls were ugly. "We put a line on the walls up to a certain height and painted underneath it," says Cadorette. "We learned how to do everything ourselves. We hired someone to sheetrock this wall between the sections, but all the rest we did ourselves. Everyone learned to paint." One Sunday, the whole crew did nothing but make extension cords for the lights and equipment.

Cadorette hired a second host, Chuck Hansen, a former *Car Craft* magazine editor and mechanic. Host Elmore liked cars but admits that co-host Hansen is the real mechanic of the group. "Chuck has about 9 or 10 Chevelles. He taught me a lot about cars, and I taught him a bit about TV."

Says Cadorette, "Joe has been on TV forever. Chuck was a mechanic forever, and he's very charismatic. He was never on TV before, and he's real confident. So it's a very good mix. We work it real well."

Cadorette found *Trucks!* host Stacey David dividing his time as a professional guitarist and a part-time mechanic. "I've been building and working on cars and trucks forever. I was a pro musician in town, and I was real fortunate—I made a good living at it. I was making no money building cars. I had a shop three or four years before this came along."

The crew of car enthusiasts built the producer's table on the right as well as the other workbenches and television production surfaces and sets. All the shows are written on the set. It takes a week of 12-hour days to make 19 minutes of the half-hour show. **Phil Berg**

David believes car enthusiasts make the best how-to hosts: "If you come away from my show and haven't learned something, then I haven't done my job. I design and build all this stuff," he adds, pointing to a custom Ford Bronco with sparkling paint, a modern mud bog–capable suspension and an all-new, high-horsepower drivetrain. "The viewers want to see the real person build it. The days of hiring the TV spokesperson just to talk about it, I think, are gone. This stuff isn't that hard to do. If a guy's got a basic toolbox, he can build cars like this. We show him."

"Stacey used to play in bars that had chicken wire between him and the audience," adds Cadorette. "TV cameras don't scare him at all."

The set was finally finished in 1998. "We've kept it secret for four years—that's the way I like it," says Cadorette. The building is divided into three 3,000-square-foot sections. The section at the rear of the building is the *Horsepower TV* set, distinguished by its

The Horsepower TV set occupies a third of the 9,000-square-foot garage. The numerous tools and their chests were donated by tool companies. Phil Berg

checkered floor. The middle third of the building houses two more sets—a small one for *Trucks!*, which is a dream garage in its own right, plus a large corner area with bright blue walls, where product commercials are taped. The front third of the building is full of cramped cubicles tfull of editing rooms and administrative offices that are usually empty. A sign on the front door tells the UPS delivery guy not to ring the bell because the crew might be taping.

"We never get bored with the background of all the tools," says Cadorette. "It's all candy. It's all things guys at home want and can't have. People watch the show and go, 'Ooh, I want that, and that, too.' " One problem is that because of the hundreds of tools and parts and pieces of equipment in the shop, some inadvertently find their way on camera—a distraction the producers try to prevent. "We really watch the monitor a lot during shooting because the photographers can't see everything."

The show gets a lot of e-mail complementing the checkered floor, which is made of a synthetic, rock-like compound. It gets sanded and waxed every four shows, about once every two months.

Each month, the whole crew gathers for a planning meeting, where the subjects of the shows are decided. The hosts are generally responsible for writing their own scripts, usually the morning of each day they tape the show. The object is to produce 19 minutes of finished show every week. Each scene in each show is done five times—three for practice and two with the camera recording on tape.

There are disadvantages to using a garage as a studio. "When a plane flies over, you stop. When a truck

The donated tool collection includes every power tool available as well as lifts, jacks, pumps, generators, and compressors. Phil Berg

goes by, you stop," explains Cadorette. Dedicated television studios benefit from soundproofing.

But no soundproofing can hide the roar of a rolling dynamometer with an unmuffled hot rod running at a virtual 100 miles per hour. The crew expanded the building to fit the dyno, which was donated by its maker, into the set. Its components, including the large drum roller spun by a car's wheels, are contained in a thick concrete trough the size of a car. The structure was built so stoutly that once a tornado passed through town and the entire crew crowded into the dynamometer room for safety, ready to take cover.

"I could never make a studio do what this garage does. We shoot with a whole lotta lights. Usually it's totally cluttered. Whatever is not on camera is just lying around. We shoot *Horsepower TV* for a week, until the *Trucks!* show is ready, and the next week we shoot that." All the production equipment, the producers' desk, and the worktables are on large casters so that they can be rolled to whichever set is ready for shooting. "The crew just locks themselves in here for a week and comes out with a show."

Sometimes a show that's planned doesn't work because a car isn't finished or breaks, so they have to create a new show as they go. "We'll shift gears real fast. The crew will get hurrying, and they'll get it done. I never worry about it. It's only because they like what they do," says Cadorette. "So far, this place is separate from the corporate office, so there's no one in charge out here. It's just one big team effort. Everyone knows what they're doing and what needs to be done, and they do it. I don't need to be a boss. It's wonderful."

21

Mark Lambert

The Preservationist

Raised from the
ashes, this old
firehouse is now
a Packard hospital

ark Lambert's attorney told him he was making a bad move when he purchased an old firehouse from the city of Nashville in 1990. But Lambert had a vision.

Underneath the scattered parts and equipment of his full-time auto restoration business today is an overdesigned, overbuilt concrete structure with ceramic and porcelain tiles and steel fixtures. It was built this way in the early 1930s, after the original wooden building burned down when a fireman left a coffeemaker turned

Previous page: Mark Lambert's garage originally was a fire station, built in the 1930s. He purchased it at a city auction in the 1990s and later found out that the building was worth much more than what he paid for it. Phil Berg

on during a run. The city wanted to make this firehouse fireproof, so no wood was used in the reconstruction and even the roof was made of slate.

Lambert installed lifts in the spaces where two fire trucks used to reside. A half-dozen cars needing work are parked outside and in a basement. Phil Berg

The rebuilt firehouse became obsolete when a modern, replacement fire station was built just a block away in the late 1980s. At the time, Lambert, who restores classic American and British cars, was looking for a place to work on cars full time. Lambert spent his years following college in what he calls a "corporate job." "I was an English major, and I always missed working on cars, so when I had a chance to go full time and do it, I jumped on it."

The rebuilt firehouse has a spacious front office, a full kitchen, and a pantry. It also has four large basement rooms, including a community center that had a small theater stage. The first floor of the single-story structure has two bunk rooms, two large shower rooms, and a dressing room with lockers. As many as 17 firefighters at a time lived in the building from the 1930s to the late 1980s.

Lambert thought the building would make a great shop when it was put on the auction block in 1990. The sealed-bid auction had a minimum bid of $50,000, but when Lambert started inquiring about the auction date, he found that it kept changing. "It seemed to be a very tight, mayor's brother-in-law kind of deal," he recalls. So Lambert had a friend find out what the final day of the auction was and showed up at the last minute with two bids, a low one and a high one. Since the auction room was full of people, he decided to submit his high bid, which beat out all the other sealed bids. "I tried to be as friendly as I could because they were a little angry that I bought it," he says.

When he won the bid, he went to his local bank, and the loan officer told him the property was worth about three times what he paid. "It was the greatest feeling," he remembers. "I could turn it over tomorrow, but I won't."

After he bought the property, Lambert lived in it alone until he married in 1996. Then he and his wife moved into a house in the neighborhood. "When I lived here, it was cleaner. Now, every room becomes a build room when you're around cars," he explains, noting that his former

The narrow stalls keep tools—ranging from antique wrenches to the latest digital analyzers—near at hand. **Phil Berg**

Lambert doesn't specialize in one make and is as passionate about this Austin-Healy project as the Packards he keeps alive. For his projects, Lambert uses some of the workbenches that came with the fire station. Also included were a full kitchen and a small theater stage in the basement. Phil Berg

living room is where he rebuilds transmissions, and parts for his clients' cars are stacked in all the other rooms.

"When you're in this business, you've got to have a lot of parts around. There was a time when I didn't really know the floor plan. I'd go down to the basement and find a room I'd never seen before. They used to use it as a bomb shelter in the 1950s. I saved all the old fire equipment from the 1930s. The older firefighters from the new station down the street come by and tell stories about some of it."

Like a lot of buildings in Nashville, this one sits on a layer of bedrock, so the massive concrete walls and ceilings have never developed any cracks. "Eventually, I'd like to do a full blown restoration and keep it much more firehouse-looking," he adds. "I just love the look of the ceramic tile."

Lambert Auto has about 135 customers, who own a total of 210 cars. Twice each month, he rebuilds an engine, most frequently Packard engines from the 1940s. "I just did a '41 Cadillac engine three weeks ago," he says.

Half the cars he works on are American classics, and half of those are Packards. The other half are more modern—British sports cars such as Healys and Jaguars, and even some new cars his customers bring in. "That's why you walk around my shop and see the 1930s hand tools and this Snap-on computer diagnostics system," he explains.

The shop has no sign outside, and the phone number is unlisted. "My most representative situation is a customer [who] brings in a car in that's been in storage all winter. He'll want it prepped for a show or the Colorado Grand rally or something, or maybe he's going to run it in a vintage race. I'll do all of the prep work," he says. Lambert's happy to remain at his current level of steady mechanical work, with the engine diagnostics machine the only computer in the shop. All his invoices and work orders are handwritten, hanging on a wall.

Lambert also belongs to the group of enthusiasts who have a genetic connection to cars. The name Lambert Auto is the same one used by Mark's grandfather, Charles Lambert, a race team owner and car dealer in Indiana in the 1920s. "I grew up in a long lineage of automobile enthusiasm. My grandfather got us going. He campaigned a team of Ford-based cars into the 1930s," Mark says.

When Mark's father was young, he tagged along to the dirt-track racing events and even rode around the Indianapolis Speedway in the mechanic's seat of a race car before a race in 1930.

"My dad, who is 78, grew up with this and encouraged all five of us boys and two girls to fool around with cars. There were always cars around as far back as I can remember," he recalls.

Packard Clipper he drives, too. In back of the firehouse is a 1941 Packard parts donor and two MGs—one a parts car, one a customer car. There's a rare 1941 Chrysler Imperial and a 1938 Chrysler in which Lambert travels to swap meets.

"Everything comes through here, from Stutzes to Auburns," he says. "I was probably 20 before I figured out that the stuff that America built in the 1930s and 1940s was the best stuff anybody ever made. Maybe not the fastest or most efficient, but the durability and the value were amazing. If you look at the conditions that these cars operated in, new cars wouldn't survive on 1930s roads. There's no difference between an old Packard suspension and a modern off-road suspension."

Lambert's first car was an MG TF, which he bought when he was just 13 and sold in 2000 to one of his customers. He raced an Austin-Healy in club races and has worked on customers' Lancias and Alfas.

"I like fixing cars," he explains. "And I like driving them when they're fixed. Driving and working on them go hand in hand. It's a central experience driving a car. Most people don't realize that. They just live with the way their switches feel—that horrible plastic feel. They drive these pod things that the industry is making today. The new cars go a long way for a small amount of work, but to me it's degrading."

Lambert feels a duty to restoring old classics and keeping them running. "Guys that got into the hobby in the 1940s and '50s are moving out of the hobby now. You've gotta get as much of this as you can before it evaporates. All the guys that made the 1930s cars are dead. All the guys that made the decisions that made those cars are dead. All those of us in the hobby now

A dozen cars are parked inside and outside the firehouse. Underneath the kitchen is a '55 Jaguar that Lambert uses to get around town. "It's just the best little commuter. There's nothing like the feel—terrific kind of center of gravity, the way the switches feel, the way the doors drop closed." Next to the Jaguar is a convertible

Lambert is rebuilding this Packard, owned by one of his 135 clients, just outside the door of his former living quarters. Phil Berg

want to do is preserve what was happening then.

"I want to know what mindset came about to make these cars, what were they originally intended for, how do we keep them happy, how do we keep them surviving for the next guy. The guys that are around 28 years old are just starting to get into it, and you can tell because Model A prices are starting to go up. Younger folks are buying them."

Just like the firehouse where they are repaired, these American classics are solidly built symbols of a bygone time, Lambert says. "They didn't have to build them that good. It was the right way to do it. It wasn't always a competitive necessity to build a car to last 40 years. That's why I like working on these things and having them around me. It's such a reflection of the integrity of the guys who made them."

22

Dan Scully

A Shrine to the Gods of Fuel

A philosophical
architect builds
a temple devoted
to racing cars

Dan Scully found an unassembled Quonset hut in the 1980s and blended it with his image of what a garage should be. The result is a temple to the gods of speed, he says. It was created out of a need for a race car shop, part of a collection of three buildings that are Scully's home in New Hampshire. Finished in 1990, the garage faces west, which is significant for Scully: "All of the mythology in this country is heading west."

Scully likes to name the buildings on his property. The monikers he has given these structures include: the Route 101 Two-Lane Highway Home, the Four-Cylinder Garage, and the Temple of Gods of Speed. Jeff Hackett

Previous page: Dan Scully's Four-Cylinder Garage makes a dramatic spectacle when lit up at night. Joanna Morrisey

Scully, an architect by trade, had enough Quonset hut raw materials to build a structure 20 feet square, but he decided that wasn't big enough and that it wouldn't accommodate two large garage doors. He visualized the starting ramp at the Mille Miglia race in Italy and wanted the garage higher than the ground so that he could build ramps similar to those used in the race.

At the time the garage was built, Scully and his son planned to race two Volvos in vintage club events and intended to keep them in the garage. Having two doors and two ramps would remind him of the two leaving the start of a mythical race, heading west: "We would be racing each other into the day."

He split the 20-foot structure into two 6-foot sections for the sides and used the remaining 8-foot section in the center, which sits between two sets of 10-foot double doors. Then he bridged the space between the center and each end section with a shed roof. Total length stretches to about 40 feet—enough room to prepare two race cars.

The two large front doors ride on metal tracks. To hold up the door headers, Scully made four 8-foot-tall wooden columns shaped like giant engine connecting rods, topped at the piston ends by 55-gallon drums.

"I was fortunate as a kid to spend some time on an ocean liner and was most impressed by the engine room, where you could actually see the connecting rods in action," he explains. "It was chance for me to do something on the same scale. So it's a four-cylinder garage."

Scully installed an antique Mobil gas pump on the roof, as a shrine to the gods of fuel, he says. "Whenever

Right: Mounted up high is the antique Mobil gas pump. Wayne Fuji

Scully races a Volvo 544 in vintage club events and has an affinity for the shape of its body. It reminds him of the 1942 Ford fender he drew repeatedly in high school. Over the bays where the cars are parked, daylight floods the rafters through translucent skylights. Windows at the sides of the building allow more light in. Jeff Hackett

you hold something in high regard, you remove it from its current context and elevate it. I call it a gas pump for a dirigible, and I sort of wanted to have the gas pump be a madonna raised up high."

On the walls inside the garage are license plates from around the country, but they are symbolically arranged, with eastern states on the east wall, leading to western states on the west walls, the direction the garage faces.

The floor is hardwood, which Scully admits is not the best choice for vehicles that leak oil, yet it gives the garage the charming feel of a granary or other rural outbuilding. "It has housed the working and campaigning of four different race cars, and that's its main purpose. That's what it was designed for," says Scully. "I don't put

Ever since Scully saw a Volvo compete in the Acropolis Rally in Greece, he's been a fan of racing Volvos. Jeff Hackett

The garage is crowded with memorabilia, tools, parts, and vintage signs. Jeff Hackett

which is again a temple kind of thing. It's bathing the cars, the steeds, in light."

Scully has been a racing fan since he was 12 years old. His uncle raced in Formula Three and won the Queen Anne cup at Watkins Glen in 1950. Scully worked for his uncle and other racers in the pits. "I probably learned to read by looking at car magazines then," he says.

His first race car came much later—a Volvo P1800 he bought in 1988. He currently races a Volvo 544. His fascination with Volvos began early: "In 1957 I spent some time in Greece, when I was a kid. I saw a Volvo 444 win at the Acropolis rally, and I convinced my parents to buy one." Scully had in mind eventually turning his parents' car into a race car, but the Volvo didn't survive his brother's youthful mishaps.

When vintage racing became popular, he realized there was a place to race the old Volvos. "I knew they were beautifully balanced and that I wanted to build one and that they could be made into a good race car." At this point, Scully's son also was interested in racing, and the two built the P1800 together.

Scully says he carries photos of his race cars because "they're like children." He doesn't carry pictures of his garage because "I don't want to scare clients away." But he's done other garage-related work. He designed the paint scheme for a BMW restoration shop and the facilities for Vermont Sports Cars, a well-known rally car prep shop. He also designed a nearby Honda dealership. The front of the building matches other Honda stores, but the back of the building is a combination of concrete blocks and horizontal corrugated metal that gives dimension to the Honda blue stripe running around it. "The Honda people liked it," he says.

He's done other automotive-themed architectural projects and is currently involved in a visitor's center in New

my daily driver in the garage—it's the race prep shop. We do all the race car work ourselves, essentially."

The Four-Cylinder Garage was the last structure to be built on Scully's property. Scully explains the theory as only an architect can: "I see it very much as an art deco building. There's not another active working garage like that. I'm amazed at the number of people who do like that building. It only brings smiles. About 200 feet from the garage is a house called the Route 101 Two-Lane Highway Home."

Translucent plastic panels cover the ends of the building and also make up skylights in the roof. Again, the architect in Scully explains: "I sort of see it as a big light-filled modern version of the baths of Caracalla,

On the outside of the garage, Scully hangs license plates from western states facing west, while the license plates for the eastern states face that direction. Jeff Hackett

England, built along a river in an old railroad yard. "We re-created an old arched bridge that was over the river and then built a train-like building going underneath the bridge," he says. "It's a very active and dynamic building."

Scully's favorite garage is one he designed but that was never built—a restoration shop with connecting-rod columns similar to his own garage. The roof held a Citroen 2CV, and the skylight "looked like a highway cutting through the mountains," he says. The building would have been shaped like a vehicle. "It didn't happen, and when I look back wistfully at garages that didn't happen, that's the one I miss."

Scully's favorite car shape is his Volvo 544. "As a kid in high school, I couldn't stop drawing the 1942 Ford fender shape," he recalls. "I don't know why, but the fenders have a streamlined look to them. They stretch

back, and they're very much about wheels." Volvo used the same design on the 544, "and they must have put it on a reducing Xerox machine and got it to be about the right size. That's the genesis of the 544."

A couple of nights each week, Scully spends a few hours in his garage, working on his race cars. "It's the best therapy I get. It's a great way for me to unwind at the end of the day and make something direct.

"Racing is all about preparation. You spend very little time on the track. It's a much more immediate gratification of my competitive instincts but also of my need to make things. Architecture, on the other hand, takes years. On the car, you're always evolving and making new parts. The racing is the only thing I do that's more intense than the office, so I can actually forget about the office."

23

Guy Webster

Brand New Old Barn

A motorcycle buff
uses movie magic
to give his garage
a lived-in look

Being a graphic designer for the entertainment industry has helped hone Guy Webster's aesthetic vision to such a sharp focus that this motorcycle lover is preserving a special group of Italian bikes related by looks alone. In the 1970s, he purchased a getaway home on a small farm in the mountains of California, specifically because it was close to the country's best motorcycle roads. He quickly discovered that his growing collection of bikes wouldn't fit inside any ordinary garage. A small barn on the property inspired him to build a new home for them.

"In 1977 I decided to collect motorcycles on a real scale, not just three or four but maybe twelve," Webster remembers. "By the end of the '70s, I needed a place larger than my garage to put them, so I built a baby barn, and as the collection grew, so did the barn. It kept growing, until I finally stopped the collection at 60 bikes. I was buying bikes and just not selling them. They were pristine condition, one owner, less than 5,000 miles on any bike."

On the 16-acre ranch, the existing barn was too small for his collection, he recalls, "So we re-created it and expanded it. It's all heated, air conditioned—you could live in it. I built it myself. I built the barn; I built the house."

Other touches he added didn't exactly follow the barn motif: "We put in the checkered floor, and then I just painted it with epoxy. And I kind of like it because it's easy to clean."

The modern floor helps when Webster opens up the garage and his property to gatherings of motorcycle clubs every couple of months. "The garage nickname is the Barn, and people come from all over the world to see what stuff is in the Barn," Webster says. He rolls most of his bikes out onto his driveway, to make more room for people to walk through the barn.

Approaching from the road, all a visitor sees is the back of what looks like an old barn. **Bill Delaney**

Previous page: Large shelves in the back of Guy Webster's barn display special bikes he doesn't often ride. Webster built the barn on his hobby farm near coastal mountains in central California. **Bill Delaney**

He also encourages visitors to arrive on their own bikes. "We just had a big show, with a hundred people here. Mostly they're from bike clubs"—although, he says, "the 300 we had last year was too many. I've had them come in from far away, including Korea. I put the bikes out here and move my trailer, and then some people bring their bikes, and sometimes there's a hundred or two hundred bikes in the parking lot."

Webster's gatherings started small, and their popularity spread by word of mouth. "People have been coming

back for 20 years—the BMW club, the Ducati club, the Norton club," he says. "They just ride in. The dates get posted on the Web—it's open to everybody."

Being in a rural area, Webster didn't find many limitations to how big he could build his barn. The local codes allowed him to build a barn that could be large enough for his 100-plus bikes, as long as the structure wasn't meant to live in. Given those parameters, Webster expanded the barn four times as his collection grew.

With 70 motorcycles, all running, all available for rides on the country's best motorcycle roads, Webster has stopped adding bikes to his collection. "The first structure could hold about 40 bikes. By the time I finished adding on to it, it got up to 80 bikes. Now I'm down to 70. I'm trying to get down to 60. How? The bike in the front there is only worth $3,000, and others are worth $50,000. You have to let the lesser bikes go."

Webster works as a designer for the film and music industries, and he used techniques from the film business to make the new barn look old. "I used old siding. I distressed the barn to make it look old. The bird shit I painted on. You see all the spider webs? They were actually painted on in the beginning, to make it look old. It's a lot of fun, but I wanted to keep it in line with my country house. There's light from the sky windows. I figure if I ever sold it, I would sell it to a car guy."

Webster had built a conventional garage for his family's cars when he built his home in 1975, and a workshop behind it has become his office and restoration shop. "This is the finishing room," he calls it. "This is where the hogs were kept when I bought the property. Then I turned it into the workshop. When I'm here, this is my office, so I'm here quite a bit during the day."

A 1973 event started Webster's obsession with Italian motorcycles. "Back in 1973, I was living in Florence. I was always into motorcycles, owning motorcycles. Not many—I had two, I think." He knew a local motorcycle dealer, who one day explained to him that the Italian motorcycle industry was in the throes of one of its many financial crises. This one was due to the boom in popularity of Hondas and Kawasakis.

"He took me downstairs, underneath this beautiful shop in Florence, with a typical vaulted ceiling from the Renaissance, and there were 40 motorcycles lined up along this long corridor, 20 on each side. He said, 'I can't sell these things—everybody wants Japanese.' They were the most beautiful Ducatis, Laverdas, MV Agustas, all the great stuff."

The Italian bikes were selling in other European countries and even in the United States, but Italian riders were smitten with the new Japanese bikes. "I looked at this beautiful lineup in this church-like setting and said, 'One day, if I ever have any money, I've got to have these bikes.' "

The fake cobwebs that adorn this eagle were made using Hollywood-style techniques.
Bill Delaney

Inside the restoration shop, Webster inventories the 10 bikes he's working on. "These are the factory racers—some are works racers, and some are over-the-counter. This is a factory Parilla Grand Sport, in original condition, and it's unrestored. The reason it looks so good is the fairing has never been on it. This is a Ducati that we're still finishing. It's very rare—a 450 Desmo. It's a factory racer from 1970. All the Ducati singles were raced. I have every bike that the classics started—that's what I did. So I'm actually not looking for any bikes.

"This little collection here is the top bikes of the 1950s and 1960s, that somebody could buy and go racing. You could buy the factory race bikes over the counter and go racing. Phenomenal. These are road bikes, but they're also race bikes. The Italians raced with lights in the 1950s. When bikes are original, I clear coat them. Keeps the air away. One was at the Guggenheim show for three years."

Back in the barn, Webster elaborates further on which bikes he selects. "All the Ducatis are here, up to the last great Ducati period—up to the new ones." At one point, Webster owned almost 160 bikes, but he sold almost a hundred, mostly bikes of the 1980s. The remaining bikes he categorizes into two collections: "From 1950 to 1980 are all the important street sport bikes, ending with the 1979 Mike Hailwood Replica. The second collection is the race bike collection from 1950 to 1970. That's 20 years of Italian race bikes.

"The '50s race bikes were raced on the street city to city. They were the most successful races in Italy because if you won one of those, the sales of your bike would go way up. They raced from Bologna to Florence and Milan to Taranto—those were all street bike races. They were actually factory race bikes with lights. They are the most gorgeous bikes I've seen.

"People have talked about buying my entire collection, and I'm not averse to it because I could do it all over again," he says. "I ride at least once a day when I'm at home. I don't ride in Los Angeles. I only get around on my

The rarest race bikes are kept in the restoration shop, which is about 100 yards from the barn. **Bill Delaney**

motorcycles in the summer—I don't use a car. I take major trips, 3,000- to 4,000-mile trips all around the world, two or three a year. We did Mexico to Peru to Costa Rica, across the U.S. and Canada, Europe, Morocco. Bikes have been part of my life since I was 16, and I'm 63.

"You have unadulterated roads here—beautiful roads that go on for hundreds of miles. That was why I chose it as a weekend house, but it became my full-time house." Even though Webster has had the barn for more than 25 years, the magic hasn't worn off. "I'm totally enthralled by the garage. Anytime, day or night, is my most favorite time in the barn. I get a thrill anytime I walk in there—whether it's five times during the day, it makes no difference."

24

Brock Yates

Parking in History's Shadow

A carriage house
becomes home
more than history

Anyone with a mild interest in cars in the United States has heard of Brock Yates. Noncar people may remember him only from his cameo appearance in the 1981 movie *Cannonball Run*, a Hollywood free-for-all loosely based on the outlaw highway race Yates created in 1971. But he's been a fixture in *Car and Driver* magazine for three decades, and he's been reporting auto racing events on television since 1976 with CBS as well as from the early days of cable television. He's written books about becoming a racing driver, about the decline of the auto

industry, about Harley-Davidson motorcycle culture, and about legendary exotic car "commendatore" Enzo Ferrari.

Yates acquired the nickname "Assassin" for scathing reviews he wrote about new cars he didn't like.

Originally Yates' carriage house was a horse stable. It was converted to a garage before he purchased the property in 1976. Yates' favorite cars are racers. He loves everything from the Cannonball Challenger to the Wayne Ewings-bodied Snook racer in the driveway. **Phil Berg**

Yates pulls his race cars out to tow to vintage events, and he starts the Challenger often so that it is charged and running. His latest favorite is this red Snook car. He considers the car's body man, Wayne Ewings, one of the two best body fabricators in the country. Phil Berg

His knowledge of American history comes out when he talks about his carriage house in upstate New York, originally built in 1907 as a part of a stable. It sits on a 16-acre slice of a former 1,000-acre farm.

He hasn't restored the stable, which remains in the rear of the two-story brick building across a courtyard from his house, "Farmstead." He hasn't done much to the garage, either, other than cover the original floor with rubber tile and add three modern doors and a heater. But upstairs, Yates has made comfortable living quarters for the daughter of friends from the small hamlet nearby. "One of the young women that works for my wife, Pam, in the village lives there. Our secretary has an office up there as well, so it's split."

Since Yates moved to upstate New York in 1979, he's invested locally. He owns a restaurant and a retail store in town, and you get the idea from the young staff that it's not to provide proceeds to fund his lifestyle but to provide some industry.

Yates' Don Kenyon–built sprint car, powered by half a Chevy small block, dominated its class for five years. Phil Berg

"That's been a wonderful experience. The nicest part of that whole thing is that we've been able to help a lot of young kids get a launch and get their lives together and go on up to school and learn some things," says Yates. "We probably, over 10 years, employed over a couple hundred people. We've seen a good percentage of them move through the business and go elsewhere, either into the restaurant business or back to college. A lot of the kids have gone back to college with the money they've been able to make there. It's nice in a small town to help kids and get them a start."

A large room at the end of the restaurant houses a bar called the Cannonball Pub. Memorabilia covers the walls. The lore of people using cars for their enjoyment is Yates' life.

When he found the house and carriage house garage, "I knew it would make a wonderful spot for a small collection. Even if I had $20 million, I'm not the kind of guy inclined to have 30 cars. It seemed like an ideal spot for some cars. At that point I had the Challenger, and we were living in a condo in Connecticut."

Raised in upstate New York, Yates was looking to reestablish roots there. "I love the seasons," he says. "Yeah, there's three shitty months, but I've found there's three shitty months almost anywhere you live, except San Diego."

The history of the place rolls off Yates' tongue like a rehearsed lecture: In 1814 the property was occupied, and in 1852 a house was built for one of John D. Rockefeller's business rivals, C. B. Matthews. When dealings in Pennsylvania oil fields went sour, "Matthews retreated to Buffalo, where he made a lot of money. This was his summer house." It was completely remodeled in 1909–10.

Yates believes the house was designed by Claude Bragdon, who was brought to the area by George Eastman

221

The second floor of the carriage house is an apartment and an office. Both are accessed through a separate door on the side of the building. **Phil Berg**

of Kodak fame. Bragdon later made a name designing some Broadway theaters.

The carriage house stored horses and early autos. An original naphtha-powered DC generator is still in place in the stable and was used to make electricity in the early days of the carriage house. The chestnut tongue-and-groove paneling was already installed when Yates bought the place.

The carriage house now holds a 1924 Model T-bodied hot rod with a glorious racing history, two midget racers, and a Dodge Challenger with an engine built by NASCAR

hero Cotton Owens that placed second and third in original Cannonball races in 1972 and 1975.

Yates remembers the first time he hung around a garage. "When I was a kid, I was raised in Lockport, New York. My dad had purchased an XK120 Jaguar. It was maintained by a guy named Don McArthur, and he was brilliant and had a tremendous understanding of exotic cars. All the biggies in town drove Buicks and Cadillacs, and this Jaguar was an outcast, and nobody understood what it was. There were only a few foreign cars, mostly MGs, and this one Jaguar.

"I remember watching McArthur work when I was a kid. He really had an insightful understanding of automobiles and cared about them. In the early 1950s, sports cars were oddball devices. Big Buicks and Cadillacs were status symbols, and if you didn't drive one of those, you were some kind of a square."

Yates learned to appreciate cars, but he also learned early about racing drivers. "My dad brought me home an issue of *Speed Age* magazine—that was the first car magazine I saw. Then I began to buy *Road & Track* and *Hot Rod*. My dad loved cars, too. He had owned Stutz when he was living in New York and would go to Sheepshead Bay. It had a big board track, and he always talked about watching Ralph DePalma race."

Yates loves the gusto and liveliness of racing drivers as much as, or perhaps more than, the cars they drove. What he likes even better than Ferraris is his hot rod, named the Eliminator. Jay Chamberlain, a Lotus distributor who worked for racer and flyer Frank Curtiss, began building the Eliminator in early 1950s. It was then completed and raced by Duffy Livingstone, who in 1956 replaced the flathead V-8 with a small-block Chevy engine. Livingstone started a go kart company in 1957 and elevated that sport to such a level that there's a Duffy award for international go kart events.

The home-built Model T bucket now has a small-block Chevy V-8 in front. Piloted in 1997 at the Monterey Historics races, it pounded around the track faster than a handful of sophisticated Ferraris. Yates calls the Eliminator a junkyard dog. He bought it in 1996 and restored it.

"It's hard to understand this car, but it's really well known in southern California," he says about the Eliminator. The oil breather catch can is an old Marvel Mystery Oil can, and the coolant expands into a World War II canteen. Yates points out with terrific pleasure that the brake scoops on the Eliminator were made by slicing a World War II Japanese army helmet in half and attaching the halves to the spindles. This setup catches air and cools the drums.

Yates already owned a sprint car made by Don Kenyon and added a Snook sprint car in 2002. The bodies of the Eliminator and the Snook car were built by the two people Yates believes are the best car-body makers ever: Emil Deke, who crafted the former, and Wayne Ewings, who shaped the latter.

The Eliminator was scheduled to appear again at the highbrow Pebble Beach show in the summer of 2003. "I can't wait to see those suits walking around looking at that thing on the lawn," says Yates. "That's going to really confuse them."

Yates has a Morgan Plus 4 and a new Mini. The daily drivers fit under a four-car awning, which is only slightly practical in snowy upstate New York, where almost every carport is enclosed. The Cannonball Challenger still runs the One Lap cross-country rally that Yates created in the 1980s.

"I don't have the desire to collect many more cars," he says. "I just like to have a few that I like and care for."

Secretly, he does have a wish list: a "250F" Maserati Grand Prix racer of the 1950s and an original Lister. Both are racing cars. "I have no prejudices, and I appreciate them all. I don't love them all. Each of these things embodied desires and motivations and dreams of a bunch of people who were really interesting."

Around 1999, Yates hatched plans to re-create the stir the Eliminator started. He built a new Eliminator with a 1934 Ford body that has more room than the Model T bucket body of the original and a handmade nose replicated in high-tech carbon fiber. The new car has the drivetrain of a Viper, and in late fall weather in October 2002, it managed to get to 60 miles per hour in just 3.5 seconds and to go from 0 to 100 miles per hour and back to 0 in 13 seconds.

Its home is now nearby Riter Restoration in Rochester. "We built it, we thought we might build some more, depending how well this one does," says Yates. A good bet is that the first one will have a permanent home in Yates' carriage house.

Index

250GT Spyder, 15
300SL Roadster, 125
427 Cobra, 18
550 Maranello, 66
904 racer, 29
911 Porsche police car, 25
Acropolis Rally, 205
Alfa Romeo, 12, 13, 80, 83, 87
An American in Paris, 77
Batman Forever, 93
Batmobile, 93, 94
Bentleys, 47
Boyd Coddington Aluma Coupe, 87
Boy on a Dolphin, 182, 183
Boyer, Herb, 16
Brilando, Joe, 14, 16
Bugatti racers, 44
Buick Roadmaster, 48
Cabriolet, 70, 71
Cadillac convertible, 94
Cadillac, 94, 148, 149, 152, 153
Cadorette, Don, 186–191
Candy Store, 12–19
Cannonball Challenger, 218, 219, 223
Cannonball Run, 218
Capital Car Store, 92
Car and Driver, 6, 150, 218
Car Craft, 186
Carrera II, 29
Catallo, Curt 176–138
Chamberlain, Jay, 223
Chevrolet Belair, 77
Chevy Cameo, 93
Chevy convertible, 94
Chevy Impala, 87
Chrysler 300, 15
Chrysler Imperial, 48
Classic Car Restoration Center, 92, 94
Cobra, 130–135
Colberg, Sid, 16
Cole, Robert, 14
Coppola, Francis Ford, 161, 162

Corvettes, 93, 69, 153
Crane, Larry, 6
Curtiss, Frank, 223
David, Stacey, 186, 187
Deke, Emil, 223
Delage, 77
Delahaye, 72, 76, 77, 165
Deuce Coupe, 176, 177, 180
Dodge Challenger, 222
Don Kenyon–built spirit car, 221
Douglas, Kirk, 158
Duesenbergs, 44, 47, 51, 44, 64, 66, 93, 95, 162
Duryea, 93
Eliminator Mark II, 223
Eliminator, 216, 217, 223
Elmore, Joe, 186
Ewings, Wayne, 223
Ferrari 375 America Vignale, 15
Ferrari 375, 182
Ferrari, 55, 165
Ford coupe, 66
Formula Three, 206
Gable, Clark, 66
General Motors, 42
Gold, Stanley, 21–29
Goodwood race, 69
Gross, Ken, 6, 98–103
GTS Ferrari, 125
Gulf Wing, 67, 69
Hammerstein, Bill, 6, 104–111
Hansen, Chuck, 186
Head, Russell, 14
Hemmings, 179
Heumann, Jules, 16
Higgins, Chuck, 6, 112–119
Hill, Walter, 30–39
Hoffman, Max, 39
Horsepower TV, 184–191
Hot Rod, 223
Hummer H2, 42
Jaguar E-type, 198
Jaguar XK120, 35–37, 39, 126
Jaguar XK140, 33, 34, 163
Jaguars, 32, 34, 37

Juchi, Bernard, 48
June California Classic, 109
Karmann Ghia, 183
Kelso, John, 43–45, 47
Lambert Auto, 197
Lambert, Charles, 197
Lambert, Mark, 8, 192–199
Leno, Jay, 8, 40–51
Lincoln Continental, 163
Livingstone, Duffy, 223
Lola T70 racer, 182, 183
Loren, Sophia, 182
Maserati Grand Prix, 223
Massman, Bruce 52–61
McCoy, Peter, 120–127
Mercedes 540K, 14
Mercedes, 66
Meyer, Bruce, 62–69
MG, 165
Mille Miglia, 69, 80, 87
Model T fire truck, 144
Model T hot rod, 156, 157, 165, 222
Monte Carlo, 29
Morgan, 51, 120, 121, 125
Motorcycles, 214
MR2, 168, 169, 171
Mullin, Peter, 70–77
Mulsanne Straight, 29
Mustang convertible, 144
Owens, Cotton, 222
Packards, 51, 55, 66, 67, 93–95, 163, 197–199
Park, Lynn, 128–137
Pebble Beach concours, 66, 69, 77, 223
Pepp, Buddy, 138–147
Petersen Museum, 66, 69, 74, 100, 109
Petit Le Mans, 25, 29, 69,180
Pierce-Arrows, 162
Pierson Brothers coupe, 62, 63, 66, 69
PM Magazine, 186
Porsche 356, 66
Porsche Gmund coupe, 180

Queen Anne cup, 206
Road & Track, 223
Sales, Bob, 43
Scully, Dan, 200–207
Sherman, Don, 148–155
Sparks, Tom, 156–165
Specialty Equipment Market Association, 103
Speed Age, 223
Speedster, 125, 183
SS90, 35
Stanley, Dean, 6, 166–173
Sting Ray, 148, 149
Studebaker Golder Hawk, 144, 147
Studebaker President, 163
Studebaker Skylark coupe, 91
Stutz, 51, 55, 60
Super Seven, 169, 171
Sydorick, David, 8–87
Talbot-Lago, 74, 77
Targa Florio, 29
T-bird, 87, 144, 147
Testarossa, 69
The Racers, 158
Triumph, 155
Trucks!, 186, 189, 191
Tryon, Lorin, 16
Tucker, 160, 161
Typhoon, 108
V-12 roadster, 36
Volvo 444, 206
Volvo 544, 204, 206
Volvo P1800, 206
Watkins Glen, 206
Wayne Ewings–bodied Snook, 218
Webster, Guy, 208–215
Williams FW12, 17
Wiseman, Al, 8, 88–95
Yates, Brock, 216–223
Z06 Corvette, 48